THE BITCOIN TUTOR

Unlocking The Secrets of Bitcoin

Marc A. Carignan

"The Bitcoin Tutor" and The Bitcoin Tutor Logo are copyrights of
The Bitcoin Tutor
Published by The Bitcoin Tutor
www.thebitcointutor.com

ISBN-13: 978-0-9798649-1-9 (Paperback edition)
Digital and audio editions also available

10 9 8 7 6 5 4 3 2 1

Carignan, Marc A., 1963-
The Bitcoin Tutor: Unlocking The Secrets of Bitcoin

This book is available at quantity discounts for bulk purchases. For information, please contact The Bitcoin Tutor by email at
info@thebitcointutor.com.

CONTENTS

4. TRADING BITCOINS 77

Marc A. Carignan

INTRODUCTION

THE PURPOSE OF THIS BOOK

The Bitcoin Tutor is dedicated to assisting people to learn about, use and profit from cryptocurrencies, the future of money. For those brave enough to lead into this new world, there will likely be handsome profits to be made. For those who love being at the front edge of something new, this is the place to be.

Rather than another book on Bitcoin technology written for computer geeks, *The Bitcoin Tutor* presents everything you need to know about getting started with Bitcoin and nothing you don't. (No offense to my geek friends!)

By the time you complete this book, you'll understand what Bitcoin really is, how to buy and sell bitcoins and how to do it safely. It's like having your own private Bitcoin tutor to help you through the process of getting started step by step.

The timing of this book is quite fitting. Bitcoins made their big debut on the world stage in 2013, gaining lots of interest and new advocates along the way. There were also its share of detractors and opponents, many in banks and government agencies who have much to lose if Bitcoin succeeds. This momentum provides you with the perfect time to learn about bitcoins and to prepare yourself with the knowledge, insights and techniques you'll need, especially while the opportunity to participate is still quite young.

Imagine if you had been presented with the opportunity to invest early in technology companies like Amazon, Apple, Google, Microsoft and others. What would your bank account look like today if you had known about the impact those companies would have on the world? What if you had invested before they became household names? Even a small amount of money would have likely grown into a handsome return.

I believe that now is the time for Bitcoin. The figurative "bitcoin ship" has left the harbor and has set sail for international success. I believe that everyone who is even the least bit connected to news and events will have heard about Bitcoin by the end of 2014. This book can prepare you to be one of the early pioneers who can profit, literally and figuratively, from the knowledge and potential rewards of Bitcoin.

Before moving on, Bitcoin and bitcoins are two different yet related things. Bitcoin refers to the network or technology and bitcoins refer to the currency. I will explain these differences in more detail shortly. Note that I use this naming convention throughout the book.

WHY IS BITCOIN IMPORTANT?

There are many reasons for the attention on Bitcoin coming from several directions at the same time.

Technology advocates consider it to be one of the most significant innovations of our lifetimes. It has the ability to revolutionize the way that value and ownership are traded, recorded and secured. Its underlying technology provides the first real digital cash and opens the door to much more.

Libertarians favor Bitcoin as it provides a medium for exchange outside of the highly controlled worldwide central bank system. These banks are given the authority by their governments to print money, regulate interest rates and set economic policy. Libertarians see this deliberate manipulation as antithesis to a free market. For this reason, this group looks to Bitcoin as the future of a market-driven and unfettered economy.

Those opposed to the often corrupt and too-big-to-fail financial system see Bitcoin as a way to disintermediate transactions, that is, to remove the friction and costs that big banks and other intermediate parties impose on business. This group sees the growing costs of managing their own money in a bank, of high interest rates on credit cards and of massive fraud protection schemes that are required to protect the system as choking the economy. Bitcoin provides a decentralized, person-to-person digital money solution that works locally and across the globe, bypassing much of this corruption.

Patriots, as a rapidly growing group of constitutionally focused Americans refer to themselves, are concerned about the growing intervention and imposition of government in their lives. They wish to be left alone to pursue happiness as they see it in their lives. This group is intrigued by the possibilities of Bitcoin as it defines a type of "private money" that can be used person-to-person. It can also keep their assets out of banks and allow them to manage their own private bitcoin holdings.

Storing their wealth in banks is a growing concern among Patriots. They refer to the government-sponsored theft that occurred in Cyprus in 2013 and are concerned that these actions could be repeated in the United States and elsewhere. For the record, 47.5% of the assets in all accounts with balances over €100,000 were confiscated to support the failing banks in Cyprus. These were called "bail-ins."

Here is another disturbing trend in the United States. Did you know that the Internal Revenue Service, the United States' taxing authority, seizes thousands of bank accounts every year without trial, proof of wrongdoing or warning? Many of these seized accounts belong to local business people who may have triggered a "suspicious activity" response with the IRS. Proving their innocence becomes more challenging when the funds they need to defend themselves, feed their family, or pay their employees, has been frozen. Patriots object to the heavy-handedness of the IRS in freezing accounts before proof is confirmed or even presented in a court of law.

A maxim is often attributed to the House of Rothschilds, a family descending from Mayer Amschel Rothschild who established his banking business in Europe in the 1760's. It is often phrased as this, "permit me to issue and control the money of a nation and I care not who makes the laws."

Whatever your reason to learn about Bitcoin, be assured that Bitcoin is changing the future of money, and in particular, the future of your money. Bitcoin transactions are like cash in nearly every way. There are no chargebacks, no need to verify personal identity, no credit card fraud to protect against and no hefty fees charged by banks for processing.

Governments cannot seize bitcoin accounts without acquiring passwords or "private keys." Although bitcoin transactions are not truly anonymous, they do provide a certain amount of privacy that helps keep transactions between various parties confidential.

The interest in Bitcoin is worldwide and growing rapidly. This book provides the opportunity to learn about and participate in Bitcoin, to discover for yourself what the excitement is all about and to determine if participating in Bitcoin is right for you.

ABOUT THE AUTHOR

I am Marc A. Carignan, a Silicon Valley entrepreneur who has participated as an early startup member of software, internet and mobile companies. I have built worldwide organizations encompassing engineering, consulting, training, sales and support functions. I have served as an executive and as an executive coach to leaders at engineering and technology companies. I have traveled to five continents and have done business in 35 countries.

Of all the roles that I play, I consider myself primarily a teacher and a motivator. I take the hard-to-understand, the technical and the challenging and make it easy to comprehend. I then help people to take the actions that will help them achieve the future they desire. I help people make the discoveries in their learning and in their thinking that help them accomplish their goals.

It was about a year ago when I first learned about Bitcoin. At that time in early 2013, the price of bitcoin was about $35. It was still quite difficult to get started with bitcoins back then. I spent many hours trying out different software applications needed to buy bitcoins at that time. I read lots of articles online, most of them very technical and rarely written for anyone except programmers and developers. Simply put, I tried to invest in bitcoins and I did not succeed. I got frustrated and walked away from Bitcoin.

Just sixty days later, in early April, I felt compelled to try again after hearing about its increase in value. Bitcoins were now trading for $100, nearly 300% of the price two months earlier. My interest in bitcoins was increasing based on the growing number of articles being published, online sites and local businesses accepting bitcoins and the buzz that was growing worldwide with new exchanges opening in the United States, Russia, China, Japan and throughout Europe. It also got a little easier to buy bitcoins with US Dollars so I gave it another try. This time it worked!

I hit many bumps along the road to learning Bitcoin including losing some money when trying to buy bitcoins with cash. I even called the CEO's of two companies that were involved in my bitcoin transaction to try to solve the problem. It was a bit of a nightmare, though as they say, "what doesn't kill you makes you stronger."

Websites that provide online "bitcoin wallets" have improved since then making it easier to buy and sell bitcoins. I have been able to distill the steps required to help friends get started. I have used my first-hand experience and my efforts helping others to write this book in a way that is clear, concise and uniquely geared to non-technical readers. I believe that this book can help you get started and be successful with Bitcoin in the same way that my one-on-one assistance with friends has helped them.

I invite you to join me on this journey into the exciting new world of Bitcoin. I truly believe that bitcoins and other cryptocurrencies have the potential to be as important and lucrative to us today as were the early days of the internet to those visionaries and investors.

Since this book cannot possibly answer every one of your questions, I have created a website to provide answers, information and additional learning resources to help you succeed with Bitcoin. Please visit *The Bitcoin Tutor* (thebitcointutor.com) website to learn more. Thanks for joining me in this journey!

If you're wondering how to say my name, it is pronounced in English like "Kerrigan". French-speaking folks may already know how to say it.

ACKNOWLEDGMENTS

I acknowledge those brave, visionary souls who started this Bitcoin phenomenon, especially the person or persons known as "Satoshi Nakamoto."

I acknowledge the early pioneers, the people who started developing, mining and using bitcoins, even spending 10,000 bitcoins for a pizza. The bitcoins used to buy that pizza would have been worth $8,160 on January 1, 2014. I hope that pizza was tasty!

I acknowledge the entrepreneurs who are building businesses in the Bitcoin economy, taking risks and creating better ways for people to manage and invest in bitcoins.

I acknowledge the investors who have built investment funds or are investing directly in new ventures, supporting the many ideas about what Bitcoin can become.

I acknowledge those who are driven politically by the possibilities of a decentralized, non-government issued currency that reduces friction in transactions, eliminates the need for large parts of the financial industry and directs the recovered investment capital back into the hands of the people to create opportunities, jobs and a more egalitarian world.

I acknowledge the visionaries and the futurists who see Bitcoin as far more than a cryptocurrency, who see the many possibilities for Bitcoin including the assignment of ownership, automated mediation, simplifying real estate and stock transactions, copyright and patent filings and many other interesting and powerful uses of the Bitcoin network.

I acknowledge all those who helped me take this project, *My Bitcoin Tutor*, from an idea to a reality. The book and its companion website will likely assist thousands to learn about Bitcoin, how to get started with it and how they can benefit from this rare opportunity.

And I acknowledge you, the reader, for taking this amazing journey into the future of your money and of so much more.

1

WHAT IS MONEY?

MONEY VERSUS CURRENCY

It was the perfect storm for the emergence of Bitcoin.

The financial world was failing. The US subprime mortgage crisis, the European sovereign debt crisis, the Federal Reserve Bank's quantitative easing program, a global recession, the stock market crash, investment company failures, bank consolidations and generalized fear about the future were raising big questions about the power vested in our leaders. Was this new financialized world of 2008 going to last or was this the end?

The details of these events are beyond the scope of this book, yet the gravity of them permeates it. All these world challenges have a common thread of "money."

Understanding money, and in particular the difference between money and currency, is pivotal to truly understanding the importance and possibility of Bitcoin as the future of money. This knowledge is required to have the basis to objectively evaluate the value of Bitcoin in comparison to other forms of money that exist today and have existed in the past.

WHAT'S IN YOUR WALLET?

If you asked most people what they have in their wallet today, most would say that their wallets contain money. I believe that most people are mistaken. Whether you carry dollars, pounds, yens or euros, these are no longer money in the purest sense. They are simply currency.

Nearly every currency in the world today is more accurately referred to as "fiat currency," meaning that the governments that issued those currencies have granted their notes and coins a value by fiat, or decree. This is in comparison to attaching something of value to back the value of these currencies such as gold or silver. Fiat currencies are backed only by faith and debt, faith that the government will continue to honor the currency and its ability to issue debt as necessary to support the value of the currency.

Although money is typically used as currency, currency is not necessarily money.

THE DAY THAT MONEY DIED

On August 15, 1971, money disappeared from American pockets when President Richard Nixon ended the international convertibility of the dollar to gold, removing the US Dollar from the gold standard. This was announced by the President to be a temporary measure in his address to the nation, with the price of gold and the official rate of exchanges remaining constant.

Like many government promises, this one was also broken. In October 1976, the government officially changed the definition of the dollar by removing references to gold from the statutes. Other countries followed suit. From this point on the international monetary system became one of primarily fiat money. I will explain the concept of fiat currency shortly.

WHAT QUALIFIES AS MONEY?

Experts agree that for currency to qualify as money it must possess several characteristics that currencies alone do not. A currency must be a store of value and maintain its purchasing power over long periods of time to qualify as money. These particular reasons help to explain why ancient civilizations favored gold and silver for thousands of years.

Many economists consider there to be seven characteristics that are required to designate currency as money. Although currency shares many of these features, money must include all the following:

- Unit of Account
- Medium of Exchange
- Portable
- Durable
- Divisible
- Fungible
- Store of Value

Money must be a unit of account. It must be measurable allowing accounting to be performed. Dollar accounting, for example, uses dollars and cents. Once value can be measured we can account for profits and losses, and assets and liabilities.

Money must be a medium of exchange. This allows people to avoid the need to barter goods and services with each other. The intermediary mechanism of money allows us to easily exchange value for goods and services provided. The medium must ensure that its object of exchange, typically notes and coins, are also difficult to counterfeit.

Money must be portable. The objects used as money must be easily carried and accessed when needed. Whether as notes, coins or other items of value, these portable representations are required of money.

Money must be durable. The object used as a medium of exchange must retain its sturdiness over an extended period of time. Notes printed on high-cloth paper and coins made from durable metals or metal blends are examples of durable media. They may not last forever, however they ensure extended use before needing to be replaced or refabricated.

Money must be divisible into small increments that can be used to purchase goods large and small. Rather than simply having dollars, we must have access to fractions of a dollar such as quarters, dimes, nickels and pennies to allow change to be made on the primary unit of exchange. Various note values also assist in creating change, such as $100, $50, $20, $5 and $1 bills.

When one dollar can be exchanged for any other dollar, being guaranteed that the value is the same from one note to the next of the same denomination, then we refer to the currency as fungible. Precious metals fabricated into standardized coins were primarily responsible for this development in the ancient world of money. Gold and silver previously had to be weighed for each transaction and the purity of the metal had to be estimated before these coins were minted into standard weights and purities. Today, notes such as dollars and euros perform this function. Gold and silver bullion coins and rounds, or coins without a stamped monetary value, are also fungible.

Money must also act as a store of value. This is the primary point of differentiation when it comes to currency versus money. Notes were actually considered claim checks when first introduced in most countries. They laid claims to gold or silver deposited into people's accounts held on their behalf by banks. As gold and silver in any large quantity is quite heavy, these claim checks allowed people to conveniently trade for goods and services. The claim checks became the first paper money as they were bearer instruments, allowing the holder of the claim checks to withdraw gold or silver, effectively backing the value of the paper. When these notes were actually backed by something of value such as gold and silver, they were actually money.

WHAT ARE FIAT CURRENCIES?

Dollars, euros and nearly every national currency today do not fully meet the definition of money described above, and in particular, they do not meet the store of value requirement. Since the notes are no longer backed by items of value such as gold or silver, they are just paper and bits of inexpensive metal. These currencies, issued by governments and granted value by government decree, are referred to as fiat currencies, or sometimes simply as "fiats."

Fiat currencies are great for governments and policy makers. To stimulate an economy, more currency is generated. To fund a war, more currency is printed. To deliver on campaign promises of jobs and economic activity, again more currency is created. However, there's a cost to all this printing.

Major countries today have central banks, like the Federal Reserve Bank, the Bank of England or the European Central Bank (ECB), that are actually privately-owned banks. Although governments have the authority to print money, this central bank model requires that governments assign this privilege to the central banks and then borrow money from these banks. Not only is the money fiat but the money is borrowed into existence.

To learn more about this concept, search online for the keyword phrase "fractional reserve banking." If this idea is new to you, you will be amazed.

Inflation always results from increasing the currency supply and creating additional debt to fund its creation. When there are more dollars vying for the same goods and services, prices go up.

It wasn't that long ago in the US when a blue-collar worker could support his family of two children and a stay-at-home mom for his weekly take-home pay. This money allowed him to buy a modest home, an automobile and all the necessities of life. Mom could stay home and raise the children, care for the home and prepare meals.

Compare that with today's reality of two working parents living paycheck-to-paycheck in fear of losing their jobs, which could lead to the loss of their house, their cars and their belongings despite having paid for these items with debt over many years. It's a very different world today due in large part to many years of government borrowing, uncontrolled spending and the loss of buying power created by the inflation that came with it.

COMMODITIES GIVE MONEY VALUE

Items of intrinsic value, such as gold and silver, are referred to as commodities. Commodities require human or machine labor to be mined, extracted, farmed, ranched or raised. Copper, oil, wheat, cattle and pork bellies are examples of commodities that are valued and traded worldwide.

The value of commodity-backed currency is based on the commodity's value and its scarcity. The value of these commodities is based on its utility function and desirability. Food items have a utility function that keeps us fed and healthy. Oil keeps the world powered and moving along. Silver is used in medicine and electronics. And gold is highly valued for the beautiful jewelry that can be crafted based on millennia of human culture.

There is only so much gold and silver above ground and only a certain amount can be mined each year. Only so much oil is extracted, only so much wheat is farmed and only so many pigs are raised each year. This scarcity keeps the money (or shares or futures contracts) that represents these commodities valuable.

When governments need more of a commodity like gold to generate more money, it limits the amount of currency that can be printed. Additional currency that is printed must correspond to a greater quantity of gold that is mined and held in reserve, or to an increase in the price of gold needed to support the additional currency. Only in this way can currency remain as money.

Gold-backed currencies are not typically backed 100% by gold, yet even 30%-40% gold backing gives them enough value to limit runaway currency creation. The Swiss franc was probably the last gold-based currency in the West. The law requiring that 40% of the currency be backed by gold reserves ended on May 1, 2000.

By limiting the amount of currency that can be created over time, commodity-based currency values tend to remain high while inflation levels remains low.

WHY GOVERNMENTS LIKE FIATS

History shows us that most countries have used commodity-backed currencies over the centuries. This practice generally comes to an end as governments determine that they need access to more money. A main reason for this need historically is to wage war. Although we often hear stories about the profitability of war, in truth war is only profitable when debt is created. Printing unlimited amounts of money requires it to shift from value-based money, or currency backed by commodities, to debt-based money, or currencies backed by borrowing. This change is only possible when shifting from true money to fiat currency.

This transition to fiat is the beginning of the end for any currency. Every country in history that has created a fiat currency has seen their currency devalue to the point of worthlessness without exception. The average life expectancy for a fiat currency is also quite brief at just 30 to 40 years according to monetary scholar Edwin Vieira. Following this collapse, the currency of the nation must be rebuilt from the ground up.

The US Dollar became fiat in 1971. Adding 30 to 40 years for its anticipated lifespan brings us to between 2001 and 2011. For the Euro, a fiat currency introduced by the European Union in 1999, the lifespan is anticipated to last between 2029 and 2039, yet many economists doubt that it will actually last that long.

Despite the 30-40 year average, the US Dollar continues to be traded to this day. Experts believe that the US Dollar's world reserve currency status has extended its lifespan. This unique privilege that the world has bestowed on the United States is quickly coming to an end as countries bypass the US Dollar in favor of direct trading in their own countries' currencies.

The massive Federal Reserve Bank program of "quantitative easing," a monetary policy that effectively authorizes the Federal Reserve to issue US Treasury Bonds, or borrowed money, on behalf of the US and then to buy them back along with purchases of troubled assets from other banks, has allowed the US to pay its bills without having any value to back the additional currency. Again, this currency is borrowed into existence. The currency is created without the need to contain its quantity as there are no commodities backing the currency, and therefore nothing to limit the amount of printing that occurs.

Fiat currencies always come to an end. History has shown that fiat currencies never work for an extended period of time for any nation. When we see governments turning up the printing presses and creating massive amounts of additional currency, we can be assured that the end of that currency is near.

Many Americans that I speak with find this hard to believe. They have experienced an extended reign of the dollar and its relative stability even beyond its expected lifespan. Could the dollar actually fail? In fact, I believe it already has.

The medication called quantitative easing that is pumping debt into the economy will only prolong the currency's life, not save it. Continuing down this path will only make the problem worse when the day of reckoning arrives. A change is coming to the US Dollar and every major world currency. I also believe that this change will happen in most of our lifetimes.

Let's look at two 20th century examples of fiat currencies meeting their ultimate demise, starting with Germany in the early part of the century and Zimbabwe (previously Rhodesia) in the latter part. I invite you to look for similarities between these two countries' experiences and the events happening in the world today.

GERMANY'S WEIMAR REPUBLIC

In 1919 following World War I, Germany created a republic to replace its previous imperial government. Referred to as the Weimar Republic by historians, named for the city where the constitutional assembly took place, the official name for this country was the German Reich.

Inflation was growing rapidly in the early post-war years yet the government continued to print currency with the knowledge that this would simply accelerate the growing cost of goods. The German Reich had war reparations to pay and so it needed to continue printing to create enough currency to settle its debts.

Most of Germany's war reparations were never fully paid despite their policy of money printing. The government began defaulting on payments instigating French and Belgian troops to take control of most German mining and manufacturing companies by 1923. Strikes were assembled by workers protesting this take-over, which further damaged the economy.

By the end of the same year, over 200 factories were needed to simply produce the paper required to print the currency needed by the republic. Hyperinflation became rampant. The cost of one pound of bread rose from 1 mark in 1919 to 3 billion marks in 1923. One pound of meat cost 36 billion marks. And, one glass of beer cost 4 billion marks.

In 1933, less than 14 years since the inception of the Weimar Republic, the fiat currency issued by the country was worthless and the German people demanded change. This demand led to new leadership and new political promises. It also ushered in the next chapter in Germany's history, that of Adolf Hilter's Third Reich.

ZIMBABWE'S $100 TRILLIAN NOTES

The Zimbabwean Dollar, issued in 1980 and lasting until 2009, was the official currency of the newly independent nation of Zimbabwe replacing the previous Rhodesian Dollar. Political turmoil and rapid inflation caused this fiat currency to quickly lose its value over this brief period.

Inflation was quite steady until 1998 when President Robert Mugabe instituted land reforms focused on taking land from white farmers and redistributing the properties and assets to black farmers. This policy of land redistribution disrupted food production throughout the country and virtually eliminated revenues from food exports.

Mugabe's government did what every other government does when they have a problem with their fiat currencies. They simply tried to print their way out of trouble.

The Zimbabwean government borrowed the money they needed from the Reserve Bank of Zimbabwe, their private central bank, and ordered the bank to print notes with higher face values. Hyperinflation followed within a few years reaching an annual inflation rate of 624% by 2004. In 2006, inflation surged to a new high of 1,730%.

The Reserve Bank of Zimbabwe tried to solve the problem by revaluing their currency yet was unsuccessful. The annual inflation rate then rose to 11,000% by June 2007 leading to progressively larger denominations being printed by the bank.

In just 29 years, Zimbabwe redenominated its currency three times to meet the needs of inflation. Inflation topped 3,700% during the currency's final years. Zimbabwe had issued bank notes as high as $100 trillion dollars. People were said to starve if they earned less than $1 billion dollars per day.

Zimbabwe no longer has its own currency. To this day, Zimbabwe has decided to use only foreign currency in its trading. Foreign currencies in use today include dollars, euros and pounds. Government policy makers have stated that a reintroduction of the Zimbabwean currency should only occur if industrial output improves. They appear to be waiting until they have sufficient national production value, in the form of commodities, to back a future currency.

There are many more examples, yet I selected these two as they are quite well known and have been studied for many years.

Let us now look at Bitcoin and how it fits into the world of money and currency.

Marc A. Carignan

2

WHAT IS BITCOIN?

DEFINING BITCOIN

Bitcoin is a peer-to-peer payment system and digital currency. Peer-to-peer refers to a system that does not require a centralized authority. The system operates and payments are processed in a decentralized manner, from peer to peer, or person to person.

Bitcoin was specified in a paper written by a pseudonymous software developer named Satoshi Nakamoto in 2008 and first implemented in 2009. It is the world's first cryptocurrency as it uses cryptography to control the secure creation and transfer of money. It remains unknown whether Satoshi Nakamoto is a single person or a group. In any event, this contribution to humanity is a great achievement.

Bitcoin was created as an open source software project. This allows people throughout the world to view it, copy it, use it, maintain it, verify it and enhance its capabilities over time. Think of open source as the opposite of copyrighting, where an invention is permanently placed in the public domain. It's like placing a secret out into the open for everyone to see. Its secret is not in its creation or its operation yet rather in its capabilities as I will explain.

The term Bitcoin is generally written in two ways, capitalized as Bitcoin to represent the technology and network, and written in lowercase as bitcoins to represent the currency itself. Bitcoins are created in a process called mining. This mining process allows participants, or miners, to create newly minted bitcoins.

Networked computers, referred to as miners, create new bitcoins at a predetermined rate. They also verify and record transfers of bitcoins in a public ledger called the blockchain. Payment for mining work is provided in newly minted bitcoins and in small transaction fees, which are also paid in bitcoins.

Users of bitcoins send and receive bitcoins, effectively buying and selling with these bitcoins, by using software on a personal computer, a mobile phone or a website. Bitcoins can be generated by mining or received in trade for products and services.

Bitcoin exchanges exist for many fiat currencies, including dollars, pounds, euros and yens, allowing direct exchange of fiats for bitcoins and back again. This process is similar to the manner in which foreign currency exchange systems function where one currency is exchanged at a particular exchange rate for another.

Bitcoins are effectively digital cash, the first real digital currency, and some would argue the first real digital money.

WHAT IS CRYPTOGRAPHY?

Cryptography is the practice and study of techniques for secure communication in the presence of third parties. It is a secret code that is used to securely transmit information, across town or across the world, preventing anyone except the intended recipient from receiving the actual message. When communications are encrypted, they are converted to what appears to be nonsense, allowing these messages to flow freely between specified parties.

The possibility of message interception is quite high, yet the risk of compromising the message is low because these encrypted messages appear to be nonsense when viewed. These messages must be decrypted, or converted back to something that is understandable, to be read. The original information is considered impossible to recover without a special key and cryptographic function to decrypt these messages, even with today's supercomputers.

Governments regularly use encryption methods that involve mathematics and sophisticated computers to make their own communications secret to all but the parties intended to receive them. In World War II code-breakers worked tirelessly to try to break enemy codes so that they would know in advance of troop movements and enemy plans.

Intelligence agencies such as the NSA, the National Security Agency in the United States, and GCHQ, the Government Communications Headquarters in the United Kingdom, continue to use cryptographic communications today and regularly attempt to break foreign nations' cryptographic communications as part of their daily operations. This is a standard part of spy work.

What Are Cryptocurrencies?

Cryptocurrencies are digital currencies that use cryptography to control the secure creation and transfer of money. Often referred to simply as "cryptos," cryptocurrencies provide a currency that can be used online in the digital world and offline in the real world.

Bitcoin was launched in 2009 as the first cryptocurrency, yet since that time, over 200 cryptos have launched worldwide. Its development is nothing short of revolutionary. Some experts have equated the invention of Bitcoin with major innovations that have occurred previously, including the launch of the personal computer and of the internet itself. What could be so compelling about Bitcoin and other cryptos to warrant so much interest and attention? The answer starts with trust.

The Need For Trust

Trust is the most important element of the current monetary system. All monetary transactions are based on trust. The buyer must offer payment and the seller must be willing to accept it. The seller expects the payment to be valid and useful for him as he is a buyer with his vendors and suppliers. The circle of trust continues on and on.

Trust is regularly challenged due to the huge economic cost of fraud. Using credit cards requires personal identification, preauthorizations with banks and may be challenged for months thereafter resulting in chargebacks to merchants. Online transactions require the full addresses, phone numbers and email addresses of buyers. The disclosure of personal information to establish transactional trust has become a huge security risk for buyers in today's economy.

Every week we seem to hear about another incident of credit card fraud or the hacking of merchant computer systems that maintain this information. This system is fraught with inefficiencies, risks and costs. In fact, Visa and Mastercard have estimated that up to 40% of their operational costs are related to fraud mitigation and resolution.

Transactions using physical currency, referred to simply as cash, generally solve the trust problem. It does, however, require verification of the currency's validity with special ink pens or other methods to prevent the seller from accepting counterfeit notes. Yet, it doesn't require the merchant to establish the identity of the buyer. Cash transactions are simple and can be anonymous.

Cash is only available for use, however, in the physical world. The use of cash for online transactions was not possible until Bitcoin.

AVOIDING THE NEED FOR TRUST

Avoiding the need for personal trust is a core element of the revolutionary Bitcoin invention. No trust is needed of either buyer or seller and no identity verification is required. At most, an email address is collected in order for a seller to correspond with a buyer and provide the digital goods purchased in exchange for their bitcoins.

Transactions in the Bitcoin network do not have to be encrypted as in the traditional banking system. The Bitcoin network avoids the need for trust and does not have to be protected from identity fraud. Cryptography and computational work together ensure the trust required for Bitcoin. Traditional banks solve this problem by limiting access, an approach which apparently has not worked very well given the growing number of credit card and personal information leaks worldwide.

Sending bitcoins over the internet is equivalent to sending cash. Bitcoins are actually pushed to the recipient. When using a credit card, you authorize a merchant to pull the funds from your account at a later time. This digital cash capability is completely new. The internet revolution has seen existing payment methods such as checks and credit cards modified for online use without any major improvements to design or security. After all, how secure is the 16-digit number that most credit cards use?

When you send bitcoins over the internet to someone, they receive ownership of the actual bitcoins rather than a promise of payment as with credit or debit cards. The ownership passes to the new party immediately. Proof occurs within seconds and confirmation within minutes. Couple this with pseudo-anonymity and we now have true digital cash. Transactions are irreversible just like cash. The seller can transfer the bitcoins back to you if they like, however, the buyer cannot retrieve his bitcoins once transferred. Again, this works just like cash.

Rather than authenticating the identity of buyers or sellers by checking identifications or by other means, bitcoins themselves are verified. Authenticating the money for validity, much like confirming that cash received is not counterfeit, is all that is required. The Bitcoin network confirms validity automatically for every transaction that occurs.

TRUST WITHOUT A CENTRALIZED AUTHORITY

The Bitcoin network operates as a peer-to-peer payment system. No central authority, such as a bank, a credit card processor or government agency is needed. This decentralized system was brilliantly designed to work in a world where trusting people is not required and every transaction is automatically verified.

A mechanism was created to verify ownership and manage the transfer of bitcoins throughout the world. The mechanism utilizes a unique concept referred to as the "blockchain." The blockchain is actually a chain of blocks, as the name implies, which contains information about transactions in the Bitcoin network. A new block of transaction history is created every 10 minutes and added to the chain. This blockchain, utilized as a public ledger of bitcoin transactions, allows a decentralized network of computers known as miners to track and verify every bitcoin transaction indefinitely.

Every transaction that has ever occurred between all parties since Bitcoin's inception in 2009 is forever recorded in the Bitcoin blockchain and freely available for anyone to review at anytime. Government agencies, investors, law enforcement, buyers and sellers may all review the blockchain.

The blockchain establishes ownership, tracks the date and time of every transaction and links each bitcoin to an owner.

Rather than using names and street addresses however, Bitcoin uses wallet addresses to identify owners. These addresses, unique sequences of letters and numbers, forever correlate ownership, duration of ownership and any transfer of ownership within the ledger.

VALIDATING THE BLOCKCHAIN

If anyone can write to the public ledger, referred to as the blockchain, what prevents a bad actor or a compromised computer from entering invalid information? The answer is consensus.

In the decentralized network of mining computers, or miners, that comprise the Bitcoin network, consensus is required to commit any changes to the blockchain. A majority of miners, currently numbering into the thousands, must agree. A full 51% of the miners would need to be acting badly and in unison to enter just one erroneous block. Trying to change previous blocks is even tougher as every subsequent block must be re-created as well. It is so difficult, in fact, that it is practically impossible.

The cost of this single change on the Bitcoin network has been estimated at approximately $500 million (USD) in computing power. Changing one or a few blocks would hardly be worth this cost. Investing this money into mining bitcoins and processing transactions is far more profitable. As you can see, Bitcoin is designed to align profit motivations with the needs of the network.

MULTIPLE CONFIRMATIONS REQUIRED

The security of the Bitcoin network is based on cryptography and network consensus among the miners of the validity of each transaction. Transactions are verified every 10 minutes with the creation of a new block in the blockchain. This occurs along with the mining of new bitcoins, which continues to gradually increase the supply of bitcoins in existence. Transactions are considered to have received one confirmation when the block that contains their transaction is completed.

Most exchanges require six confirmation, or six blocks to be created before releasing funds to the receiver of the bitcoins as a precaution against potential fraud. This means that the block with the transaction, plus five more, must be added to the blockchain. This only takes about 60 minutes, or six blocks times 10 minutes per block.

Compare this with merchants receiving funds from credit cards, which may occur in as quickly as 24 hours, but which can be contested or charged back for months later. With bitcoins, all transactions are final, just like with cash. And funds are available to the merchant in just about an hour.

Note that even before the confirmations have been received, transactions are generally considered irreversible. That is, bitcoin transactions are nearly instant. The confirmations, however, require just a little more time.

HOW TO WRITE IN BITCOIN

Bitcoin amounts are written in a similar manner to dollars and cents today. Instead of using two decimal places for cents, however, it uses eight decimal places. This allows the smallest unit of the bitcoin currency to represent 1/100,000,000 (one hundred millionth) of a bitcoin as opposed to a penny, which only represents 1/100th (one hundredth) of a dollar. We refer to the smallest fraction of a bitcoin, or one hundred millionth of a bitcoin, as one "satoshi" in homage to Satoshi Nakamoto's invention. As you would expect, multiples of these units are called satoshis.

Although very precise and highly divisible, an additional option was needed to better express so many decimal points. This is accomplished with bitcoins, milli-bitcoins and micro-bitcoins, each representing a value 1,000 times smaller than the former.

For example, if something is valued at one bitcoin, typically written as "1 BTC" using the symbol BTC that is commonly used as the currency symbol for bitcoin, this same value can be represented also as 1,000 mBTC, or one thousand milli-bitcoins. 1 BTC can also be represented as 1,000,000 μBTC, or one million micro-bitcoins, which uses the Greek letter Mμ as used in mathematics to represent a fractional amount of one millionth. So, 1 BTC = 1,000 mBTC = 1,000,000 μBTC.

Note that if your keyboard doesn't have a Mμ character, that is the Greek symbol that looks like a lowercase 'u' with a tail, simply use a lowercase letter 'u' to represent milli-bitcoins, as in uBTC.

So why does this change in notation matter? It is believed by some that the value of one bitcoin could approach $100,000 or more in the years ahead. As adoption and interest grows, and due to its scarcity with its 21 million bitcoin limit, the value of bitcoins is likely to grow substantially as more people enter the bitcoin market. Remember that both value and scarcity are necessary requirements for a well-functioning monetary unit.

If that large increase in value occurs then trying to buy something worth a relatively small amount, whether worth $20.00 or 20 cents, would require lots of confusing decimal places. At a $100,000 value per bitcoin, $20.00 would be represented as 0.0002 BTC, which is pretty confusing for most of us used to two decimal places. In milli-bitcoin, the value can be written more simply as 0.2 mBTC or even as 0.20 mBTC, which will make the dollars and cents folks more comfortable when writing the value with two decimal points.

Let us consider how to represent $0.20, that is 20 cents, in bitcoins. Again, assuming $100,000 per bitcoin, we would write 0.000002 BTC. Readability can be improved by notating this amount in milli-bitcoins as 0.002 mBTC. Expressed in micro-bitcoins, this same value would be written as 2 μBTC or equivalently as 2.00 μBTC. I anticipate that as bitcoins become more widely used that milli-bitcoins and micro-bitcoins will become a common way to express small monetary values.

As bitcoins use eight decimals of precision, the most accurate way to write the value of one bitcoin would be as the number 1 followed by a decimal point and eight zeroes, or 1.00000000 BTC. This is similar in concept to dollars and cents where it is much more common to see $1.00 written with two decimal points although $1 represents the same amount.

Figure 1: The Bitcoin Currency Symbol

A new currency symbol, the letter B with one or two vertical lines through it, is fast becoming the preferred currency symbol for bitcoins as an alternative to writing BTC. Just as the dollar sign is most simply written as the letter S with one or two vertical lines through it, this "$" symbol makes it easier than writing USD for United States Dollars. Therefore you may see either BTC or this new currency symbol used when people write in bitcoins.

ISO Currency Codes

The International Organization for Standardization (ISO), an organization that promotes worldwide standards, assigns the 3-letter codes that are used in currency trading. The ISO 4217 standard typically uses the first two letters of the currency code to refer to the country and the final letter to refer to the currency. The symbol USD refers to the United States Dollar while the JPY refers to the Japanese Yen. The ISO does not get involved in currency symbols such as the dollar ($) or euro (€) signs as many countries share these symbols.

The ISO standard also assigns codes to precious metals such as gold, palladium, platinum and silver as expressed per one troy ounce, the standard unit of measure for these metals. The

United Nations currency basket known as Special Drawing Rights (SDR) is also represented.

All non-national currencies in the ISO naming standard start with the letter "X" followed by two characters. Gold uses XAU, where AU is the chemical symbol for gold. Silver follows the same pattern by using XAG. Special Drawing Rights, although commonly referred to as SDR's, have been assigned the code XDR by the ISO.

The symbol commonly use for bitcoins, BTC, is not approved by the ISO and is likely to change in the future as it does not conform to the standard. The first two letters of the symbol actually refer to the country of Bhutan making it problematic as an international symbol. The symbol XBT has been proposed although is not yet approved by the ISO for use with bitcoins.

Currency exchange site XE (xe.com), however, has recently listed bitcoins as XBT, being the first currency exchange site to use this newly proposed currency code.

ARE BITCOINS MONEY?

Let us get back to our initial question. Are bitcoins money? Do bitcoins meet all the requirements of money or are they simply an alternative form of currency? Are they "cryptomoney," that is cryptographic money, or simply cryptocurrencies?

Money includes gold and silver coins, and paper notes that are backed by items of value, or commodities. Money is either a commodity itself as in gold coins or backed by a commodity as in paper notes that act as claim checks on gold held in reserve.

Commodities require human or machine labor to produce the items of value. Bitcoins require machine labor along with a small amount of human labor to be created.

Commodities must be valued and traded worldwide. The same is true of bitcoins.

Commodities must be scarce like the amount of gold above ground, the amount of oil that's been extracted or the food that's been grown. Bitcoins are scarce by virtue of a predefined mining limit of 21 million coins.

So, are bitcoins money? Are they currency? Or are they a commodity? It appears that bitcoins may be considered all three depending on who you ask.

Bitcoins are also traded on exchanges like stocks. Currencies are also traded on exchanges allowing dollars to be traded for euros or yens for pounds. So, are bitcoins more like currencies or more like stocks?

APPLYING THE MONEY TEST TO BITCOIN

Let us apply the money qualification test to bitcoins and see how well it fits. Remember that the seven characteristics of money are as follows:

- Unit of Account
- Medium of Exchange
- Portable
- Durable
- Divisible
- Fungible
- Store of Value

Bitcoins are units of account. The precision of bitcoins with eight decimal places allows a wide range of values to be expressed as bitcoins, allowing accountants to track gains, losses and so on.

Bitcoins are a medium of exchange as are all cryptocurrencies. Any amount of bitcoins can be transferred from one party to another, whether from a customer to a merchant or from a merchant to a supplier within the Bitcoin network.

Bitcoins are portable. It is true that cryptocurrencies are geared to online transactions, however, you can pay with bitcoins for goods and services at point-of-sale (POS) transactions with mobile wallets today. The medium of exchange may be digital, yet the portability extends to the physical world.

Bitcoins are durable. Bits of computer data representing bitcoins don't wear out. The computers that hold this information typically run for many years before needing to be replaced, yet the information that represents the bitcoins remains.

Bitcoins are divisible. Bitcoins provide eight decimal places of divisibility allowing units as small as one satoshi, or one hundred millionth of a bitcoin, to be transferred from one party to another.

Bitcoins are fungible. One bitcoin has the same value as every other bitcoin. Note that new developments in Bitcoin technology, however, may further enhance this capability in the future where bitcoins may be "colored," that is, associated with other types of value beyond what is possible with traditional currency today. Discussion of the future uses of bitcoins is beyond the scope of this introductory book.

BITCOIN AS A STORE OF VALUE

This leaves us with one final consideration. Are bitcoins a store of value? To answer this question, we should review the historical value of bitcoins since their inception.

Bitcoins were valued at less than one cent when they first began trading publicly in 2010. In fact, $0.003 represents less than one-third of a cent.

In the years that followed, the price of bitcoins rose dramatically as measured by the opening price of bitcoins for each subsequent year. At the start of 2011, bitcoins traded for $0.30, or 30 cents. In 2012, bitcoins started off the year at $5.27. In 2013, bitcoins traded at $13.30 at the start of the year. And, by the start of 2014, bitcoins opened the year at $816.00.

Figure 2: The Historical Value of Bitcoin

Date	Value Per Bitcoin*	Bitcoins Mined**	Market Capitalization
Early 2010	$0.003	N/A	N/A
January 1, 2011	$0.30	5,027,250	$1,508,165
January 1, 2012	$5.27	8,007,500	$41,639,000
January 1, 2013	$13.30	10,607,500	$143,848,308
January 1, 2014	$816.00	12,165,100	$9,827,813,254

* USD value at market open rounded to the nearest cent (except for 2010)
** Bitcoins will continue to be mined until 21 million have been created

Is the fact that bitcoins have significant value sufficient to state that it is a store of value? I believe it is not. The US Dollar has a value too, although much lower than bitcoin, yet a growing number of investors no longer consider it a true store of value either.

The dramatic increase in the price of bitcoins has caused some people to consider it to be a price bubble, much like the housing bubbles of the 1980s and 2000s or the technology bubble of the 1990s. I don't believe these are accurate comparisons, yet this is a concern for many who don't understand the intrinsic value of the Bitcoin network and its revolutionary technological impact.

Prices for bitcoins are due to numerous factors including concern about the long-term value and stability of fiat currencies around the world, investors' desires to diversify their assets and the fact that the value of bitcoins is derived from it being more than a new currency or investment vehicle but also a new technology. This aspect is more like investing in a technology stock Initial Public Offering (IPO) and tracking the rise in valuation of a new technology.

Price volatility has also been raised as a reason why bitcoins are not a true store of value. Lack of liquidity, that is a lack of a great enough number of bitcoins in circulation, has contributed to large swings in the value of bitcoin. Bitcoins surged in value from around $13 in January 2013 to over $260 in early April of that same year. One week later, bitcoins were trading for a short time at just over $50 and rose back up to $106 at the start of May. Bitcoins reached their highest value to date of $1,242 in late November 2013. By January 1, 2014, the price of bitcoins was back down to $816. This volatility is a concern to many people in regarding bitcoins as a store of value at this time.

The decentralized nature of Bitcoin is a significant part of its value. Individuals can transfer assets from person to person without intermediaries such as banks and financial institutions. Bitcoin wallets typically cannot be seized and funds cannot be withdrawn by others when taking proper security precautions. Bitcoins are also a truly international currency allowing the ability to engage in transactions worldwide with far less friction that going through intermediary banks and fiat currency exchanges. Each of these elements gives it value, yet there is one more to consider.

Cryptography is itself a hugely valuable asset. Considered as a type of munitions by most governments, cryptography is a tool of war and, in the case of Bitcoin, a tool of privacy. The privacy benefits of cryptography, of validating digital cash transactions and of maintaining a permanent and unchangeable history of all transactions intrinsically adds value to bitcoins. This is a huge advantage over fiats and benefits a free and open market.

Bitcoin is something totally new. Some have proposed the analogy of comparing physical currency to bitcoin as in comparing physical mail to email. This has some truth to it yet it oversimplifies the power and capabilities that Bitcoin provides. Cryptography, decentralization and the lack of a need to establish personal identity or trust in accepting payments are all unique and compelling reasons to declare value in bitcoins.

Regardless of whether people agree that bitcoins are actual stores of long-term value or not, they clearly have value today. This is demonstrated by the market of buyers and sellers of bitcoins. On January 1, 2014, for example, buyers and sellers were willing to trade bitcoins for $816 per bitcoin, literally 816 times the value of a US Dollar.

Think of bitcoin prices as you would share prices listed on a stock exchange. How are prices determined? Stock traders will tell you that when more buy orders than sell orders are placed, prices tend to rise. When more sells than buys arrive, prices tend to fall. News about stocks, specifically relating to the companies for which the stocks are granted, may drive prices higher or lower. Government and industry news may also drive prices. Market manipulations aside, prices are driven by demand, that is whether more people wish to buy or more people wish to sell. The same is true for bitcoin prices and exchanges.

I think of cryptocurrencies today as a new gold. Its value is determined by a consensus of people who are buying and selling bitcoins in an open market. This is a free market scenario where prices are not manipulated or regulated, but rather where buyers and sellers find a natural level for trade from day to day and moment to moment. It represents true value as determined by the people.

I believe that time will tell whether bitcoins continue to increase in value as cryptocurrencies, and whether they graduate from cryptocurrencies to cryptomoney.

In any event, this is an amazing time to be involved in the birth of cryptocurrencies.

Marc A. Carignan

3

GETTING STARTED

DON'T FORGET YOUR WALLET

It is now time to get started with bitcoins. You will need to setup a "bitcoin wallet" in order to buy and hold bitcoins. Think of your bitcoin wallet as you do the wallet in your purse or pocket. You need to keep your bitcoins safe in your bitcoin wallet as you would keep your fiat currency safe in your physical wallet. Remember that bitcoins are controlled by the person who has them, just like fiat currency. They are both bearer instruments.

Let's start with some of the common sense basics about how you should care for your physical wallet, the one with the fiats:

- Don't leave your wallet lying around.

- Make sure your wallet is somewhere safe when it's not with you.
- Don't put all of your hard-earned cash in your wallet; store some of it elsewhere.
- Be careful who you trust with your wallet.
- Create a routine to store your wallet in the same place each day so you don't forget where you put it.

There are digital equivalents to each of these common sense safety conventions. I'll discuss each as we review the different types of wallets available.

BITCOIN WALLETS

There are many types of wallets now available. Each has its own benefits and risks. Some are simple to use and others provide expert users with greater control and more complex options.

Many new companies have recently launched easier-to-use bitcoin wallets, simplifying the process of buying, selling and exchanging bitcoins. This process was previously tedious, difficult and error-prone. These simplifications are sure to increase the use and adoption of bitcoin by many more people.

The primary types of bitcoin wallets available are as follows:

- Computer Wallets
- Online Wallets
- Mobile Wallets
- Offline Wallets
- Hardware Wallets
- Paper Wallets

COMPUTER WALLETS

Computer wallets are the original wallets for bitcoins. These wallets are provided as free software that you can download and install on your home computer, whether you have a Microsoft Windows PC or an Apple Mac. Installing this software is easy, yet keeping it safe requires diligence. Computer viruses that may affect your computer can also affect a computer-based bitcoin wallet. Security therefore becomes more important when using a computer wallet.

Advanced users often prefer a computer wallet as this keeps control of their bitcoins locally on their computer. The private keys that are required to perform transactions, as needed to send bitcoins to another party, are kept locally in computer wallets. As long as you keep your computer safe, secure and backed up then your bitcoins will be safe as well.

ONLINE WALLETS

Most online wallets are quite new and provide the simplest type of wallet for most bitcoin users. Several companies around the world launched online wallets in 2012 and 2013. Bitcoin users may create online wallets hosted anywhere in the world due to the global nature of bitcoins.

Online wallets are usually free to create and are accessed using your favorite web browsers. I recommend that you access these wallets from a Windows or Mac computer rather than from a mobile device as some of the online wallet sites do not operate properly on mobile.

MOBILE WALLETS

Mobile wallets are another choice for bitcoin users. Several apps, or smartphone applications, are available. Most of these apps connect to existing online wallets. Some apps create their own local wallets as well.

Smartphones are the easiest way to bring bitcoin transactions into the physical world. Apps let you access your online wallets on the go and use bitcoins to pay for goods and services at thousands of merchants worldwide including many grocery stores, cafes and restaurants.

As of the start of 2014, Apple had withdrawn all bitcoin apps from their App Store preventing iPhone and iPad users from using bitcoins on their devices. They have done so without notice or comment. I anticipate that Apple will step forward with support for bitcoin in the near future, or some competing technology, as part of a larger strategy for digital commerce. It seems highly unlikely that Apple would walk away from the Bitcoin revolution and surrender to the competition.

Android smartphone users are in luck. Several bitcoin apps are available in the Google Play store that allow you to take bitcoins on the road. I may just have to "upgrade" from my iPhone to an Android smartphone if Apple doesn't provide support in the near future!

OFFLINE WALLETS

Offline wallets are more advanced. People who own a large amount of bitcoins require additional security. Offline wallets can provide this security. Software wallet programs such as Armory (bitcoinarmory.com) allow users to secure their bitcoins offline preventing viruses or hacker attacks from seizing their bitcoins. This offline computer effectively becomes your secure bitcoin bank.

Sending bitcoins from your offline bank is a bit more involved. A transaction must begin with a computer wallet connected online, be validated offline with a digital signature and then transferred back to the online computer wallet to complete and broadcast the transaction to the Bitcoin network. This is an advanced concept and beyond the scope of this introductory book.

HARDWARE WALLETS

A variation of the offline wallet is the hardware wallet. The first of these devices is expected for release in 2014. These devices will be small and portable. As offline wallets are typically stored on laptop PC's without internet connections they are too big and bulky to carry around in your pocket. Hardware wallets will be similar in size to the remote control device used to lock and unlock your car doors.

You only need the hardware wallet when you want to send bitcoins. This device is then used in a similar manner to the offline wallet. This is also an advanced concept and will be discussed in subsequent advanced learning resources.

PAPER WALLETS

Bitcoins stored in paper wallets may provide the greatest security. Computer, offline and online wallets often provide the capability to either backup your bitcoins or actually transfer them to paper. The information that must be stored on paper are your private keys. Like the keys to your house or your car, bitcoin private keys unlock the capability to send bitcoins from your wallet to someone else, whether in exchange for goods and services provided or to "cash out" your bitcoins into your favorite fiat currency.

Online hacking is useless in the case of a paper wallet. However, as with anything physical like cash, you need to take precautions against fire, water, loss and theft. Treat paper wallets as you would a stack of $100 bills. Put them in a fireproof safe or another location that is protected from these potential hazards.

You must also keep paper wallets away from prying eyes. These wallets are printed with the private keys required to restore your wallet online at a later date and often a QR Code, or Quick Response Code, with your key information encoded. QR Codes allow computers to easily scan in the keys required when reloading your paper wallet online in the future. If anyone snaps a picture of your paper wallet from his or her smartphone or camera then your security is compromised. Keep them secret and keep them safe.

High levels of bitcoin safety can be achieved with the various wallets options available. Safety is always a tradeoff between security and convenience. It may be safer to secure your house with a door lock, a deadbolt and a security alarm, however, it isn't as convenient as leaving the door wide open. You must take care to follow the proper guidelines for each type of wallet you may use.

CREATING AN ONLINE WALLET

Creating an online wallet is my recommendation for your first wallet. These wallets are powerful, simple and often include an exchange capability that allows you to exchange bitcoins to and from your local fiat currency. I will discuss exchanges in more detail shortly.

There are many online wallets available. Online wallets are accessed from any computer using your favorite web browser, such as Internet Explorer, Firefox or Safari. You may have multiple bitcoin wallets just as you may have multiple wallets or purses to manage your cash and credit cards.

Here are some suggestions on where to start based on your local fiat currency:

Figure 3: Online Wallets That Exchange Fiat Currencies

For This Fiat Currency...	Try This Online Wallet
United States Dollar (USD)	Bitstamp (bitstamp.net) Blockchain (blockchain.info) CampBX (campbx.com) Coinbase (coinbase.com) Coinsetter (coinsetter.com)
European Union Euro (EUR)	Kraken (kraken.com)
United Kingdom / Great Britain Pounds Sterling (GBP)	Bit Bargain (bitbargain.co.uk) Bittylicious (bittylicious.com) In Bitcoin We Trust (ibwt.co.uk)
Chinese Renminbi / Yuan (CNY)	BTC China (btcchina.com)
Russian Ruble (RUR)	BTC-E (btc-e.com)
Australian Dollar (AUD)	BTC Markets (btcmarkets.net)
Israeli New Shekel (ILS)	Bitcoil (bitcoil.co.il)

There are many more wallets yet these are a good start and are among the most popular online wallet sites worldwide. Note that *The Bitcoin Tutor* does not warrant any of these wallets, companies or currency exchange options. The choice is up to you.

Some online wallet sites also allow you to exchange between multiple fiat currencies, including US Dollars, Euros and Chinese Yuan. Online wallet companies are sprouting up worldwide. Once you are familiar with the concept, you will find that all online wallets operate in a similar way, just as all traditional online banking sites operate with a similar model.

The important point in selecting your first wallet is that it should allow you to exchange your local currency for bitcoins. This makes it easier for you to get started converting the fiat currency in your wallet for bitcoins.

PREPARING FOR WALLET SETUP

The first step is to open your favorite web browser. You can use any standard browser such as Internet Explorer, Firefox or Safari. Please perform these steps on a Windows PC or on a Mac. There are mobile wallets available for use, however, I recommend that mobile wallets be used only after your online wallet is operational.

The sign up process is similar across all online wallets. The primary requirement is to provide a valid email address. I recommend using a secure email address such as one provided by Google's Gmail. This Google service provides additional security options that can protect your security. If you already have an email address that you would like to use, you may use it to create your wallet. Avoid using shared or work email addresses as these are not as secure.

Creating email accounts with Google is free. Simply go to Gmail (gmail.com) and follow the sign up instructions if you require a new email address.

STEP-BY-STEP ONLINE WALLET SETUP

Within your browser, navigate to the online wallet website you selected, such as Coinbase (coinbase.com) or Kraken (kraken.com), by entering the web address into the browser.

Many online wallet sites are exchanges as well, as I mentioned earlier. You may see the current price of bitcoins displayed in your home fiat currency as well as several other currencies at these sites.

Various wallet sites use differing terminology. The terms "Sign In" and "Login" are synonymous. You will need to have an established wallet to use those terms. The terms "Sign Up" and "Create Account" are also synonymous. This is the first step in creating a new wallet. Click "Sign Up" now.

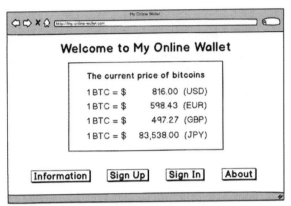

Figure 4: Sample Online Wallet Home Page

The online wallet site will request your preferred email address and a unique password for use with your wallet. I recommend that the password you select be written down on paper and stored in a safe place. You will not want to forget about or lose this information. Passwords should be at least eight characters long and include at least one uppercase letter, one lowercase letter and one number. Don't make it too easy. And again, write it down.

Figure 5: Wallet Sign Up Page

Click on "Create Wallet" or a similar button to create your first online bitcoin wallet.

The online wallet site will require that you verify your email account by clicking on a confirmation link that will be sent to the email account you specified. Go to your email account now and find this confirmation email message. Within the message you will find a link called "Verify My Email Address" or something similar. Click this link now.

Figure 6: Confirmation Email Message

Clicking on the verification link will take you back to the online wallet site. You will typically need to accept the site's user agreement next if you want to maintain a wallet with their company. Click on "I Agree" or a similar link to create a wallet according to their terms and conditions.

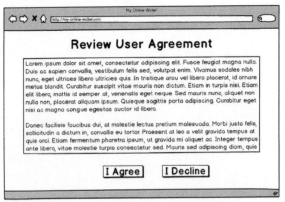

Figure 7: Online Wallet User Agreement

You now have your very first bitcoin wallet ready to go! Just click on "Sign In" the next time you visit your online wallet site home page and enter your email address and password to login.

You are now presented with your wallet home page. Several options will be available such as to buy, sell and send bitcoins.

Figure 8: Online Wallet Summary

I will discuss each of the major options in the sections ahead. First, we'll want to get some bitcoins in your wallet.

FUNDING YOUR WALLET

You will need to fund your new online wallet with bitcoins. There are generally four ways to get bitcoins into a wallet:

- You can buy some bitcoins by exchanging them for fiat currency held in your bank account.

- You can buy some bitcoins by exchanging them for fiat currency provided as cash.

- Someone can give you bitcoins if they already have some in their wallet.

- And, you can mine for bitcoins. This is an advanced concept not covered in this introductory book.

I will cover the first three ways starting with bank account funding.

CONNECTING TO YOUR BANK

Many online wallet sites allow you to connect your bank account to your bitcoin wallet. Online wallets hosted in various parts of the world allow connections to bank accounts in their home countries using their local fiat currencies. Connecting your bank account to your online wallet may take a week or more to setup. It is worth the wait, however, since this is the easiest way to buy and sell bitcoins. Funds can be easily withdrawn from your bank account when you buy bitcoins or deposited to your bank account when you sell bitcoins.

If your wallet supports bank account connections, the following steps will help guide you through the process. The ability to connect to your bank account is likely to be available under "Account" options. Expect different terminology to be used by various online wallet sites.

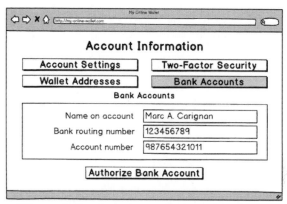

Figure 9: Bank Account Connection Setup

You will need to provide information regarding your bank account next. This is information available on a blank check associated with the account or you can request this information directly from your bank. Specifically, you will need the name on the account, the bank routing number and your account number. The online wallet provider will also expect the name on the bank account to match the name associated with this online wallet in order to make the connection.

Bitcoins do not require the identity of the person using the cryptocurrencies, yet traditional banks do. When online wallets that allow bank account connections become your bridge from the crypto world to the fiat currency world, then they will require your identity information as well. Clicking on "Authorize Bank Account" or a similar link in your online wallet will begin the process of connecting your online wallet to your bank account.

You will need to wait until the connection is made in order to buy or sell bitcoins using your bank account funds.

Although bank account transfers are the easiest way to buy and sell bitcoins, you do not have to connect your bank account to your wallet to fund you account. You can buy bitcoins with cash, you can buy them from someone you know and you can accept bitcoins from others as gifts or in exchange for goods or services. I'll cover buying bitcoins with cash in a moment.

IDENTIFYING YOUR WALLET

You can think of your bitcoin wallet as your bank account for bitcoins. You need to use your bitcoin wallet address in order for you to accept bitcoins just as you would need a bank account number to receive deposits.

A wallet address is unique, meaning that no one else has that same wallet address. This address is represented as a sequence of letters and numbers. Anyone in the world can send bitcoins to you with your wallet address. There are no national borders to be concerned about as with fiat currencies. When people send you bitcoins, they will automatically show up in your wallet.

An example wallet address is:

15etBJtqYz6wJBa1JtBdm3REe9iaAa5L5z

Note that there are upper and lower case letters and numbers. This address is case-sensitive, meaning that a capital letter is different than a lower case letter. This sequence is also very important.

Most wallets provide your wallet address within the account information section. Online wallets may file this information in different areas on their sites as well.

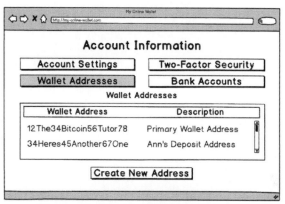

Figure 10: Bitcoin Wallet Addresses

You may have more than one address available for your wallet. This is a feature of Bitcoin where wallets may have multiple addresses. Each of these addresses refers to the same wallet, so giving out any valid address will allow people to send bitcoins to your wallet.

People often use different wallet addresses to track who sends them bitcoins, as it is easy to tell to what address bitcoins were sent. By tracking who receives each wallet address, you can easily determine who transferred bitcoins to you and who did not.

Click on "Create New Address" or a similar link to create a new bitcoin address. Many online wallets also allow you to create a brief description associated with each wallet address. This allows you to easily associate wallet addresses with their purposes.

For example, one wallet address could be marked as the "Primary Wallet Address" and another as "Ann's Deposit

Address." The first could be used generally for multiple uses and the second one specifically related to Ann's deposits.

You can simply provide the same bitcoin wallet address for every transaction as the name "Primary Wallet Address" implies. The choice is up to you.

When you want to receive bitcoins from someone else, simply provide them with your wallet address. You can select the wallet address you wish to provide then copy and paste the address into an email. Send the email to someone who wants to send you some bitcoins.

SAFELY ENTERING WALLET ADDRESSES

I recommend never typing in wallet addresses by hand. Doing so is very error prone. Wallet addresses with even one character difference will cause bitcoins to be misrouted, just as asking someone to deposit money into a bank account with one number changed will fail as well.

Always select the wallet address on your computer screen, ideally with a double click to select the entire wallet address. Copy the address by entering CONTROL-C on your PC, or COMMAND-C on your Mac. Note that you can also click on the Edit menu followed by Copy.

Create the email message you want to send to someone who wants to send you bitcoins, letting them know that you are providing them with your bitcoin wallet address for them to use to send you bitcoins.

Then paste the wallet address into this email message by entering CONTROL-V on your PC, or COMMAND-V on your

Mac. Note that you can also click on the Edit menu followed by Paste.

That is all you need to do to receive bitcoins. Now you simply need a good reason for someone to send you some!

Although copying and pasting bank account numbers is not usually recommended, doing so with bitcoin wallet addresses is much safer. People can only send bitcoins to a wallet address, not withdraw bitcoins. Bank account numbers, on the other hand, allow people to deposit and withdraw cash and are therefore less secure.

I will present how to send bitcoins shortly.

BUYING BITCOINS BY BANK TRANSFER

Buying bitcoins with funds from a linked bank account is the easiest way to acquire bitcoins. Simply click on the option to "Buy Bitcoins" in your online wallet. The screen that appears will allow you to enter the amount of bitcoins you would like to buy.

For United States based online wallets, the current price per bitcoin is provided in US Dollars (USD). Any fractional amount with up to eight decimal places may be specified when buying bitcoins. Your wallet will calculate the cost in fiat currency to purchase the specified number of bitcoins.

Figure 11: Buying Bitcoins By Bank Account Transfer

You will need to specify the number of bitcoins to buy and the bank account to use to pay for the bitcoins in the case where you may have linked more than one account. Based on the number of bitcoins you specify, the subtotal, fees and total cost will be calculated to reflect your choice.

For example, to buy one-quarter of a bitcoin, you will need to enter 0.25 bitcoins. At a price per bitcoin of $816, the transaction will require the transfer of $204 plus any fees required by your online wallet provider. These fees will likely amount to only a dollar or two.

You can easily change the number of bitcoins you want to purchase until the total cost is acceptable to you. Once you are satisfied with the pricing and wish to purchase the bitcoins, click on "Buy Bitcoins," or a similar link. Your order will be filled in as quickly as one hour to as long as a few days depending on the online wallet provider. Make sure to read the fine print to learn how quickly the wallet provider will fill your bitcoin order based on payments withdrawn from your bank account.

BUYING BITCOINS WITH CASH

Some people prefer not to connect their bitcoin wallets to their bank accounts or simply want to buy bitcoins with cash. Cash transactions will typically clear much faster than using your bank account to buy bitcoins. There are various options available depending on your home country. Two such companies are based in the United States:

- Cash Into Coins (cashintocoins.com)
- CoinRnr (coinrnr.com)

Both of these companies allow funding the purchase of bitcoins with cash deposited to a designated bank account. The bitcoins you purchase are then transferred to the wallet address that you specify.

Be aware that these sites are typically not wallet sites. They are simply cash to bitcoin exchangers. Many countries have similar services available for their local fiat currency as well.

The process is quite simple and is typically broken into three steps as follows. Note that your particular exchanger may work a little differently, yet the basic steps should be similar.

First, enter the web address of the cash exchange site you would like to use into your web browser. Expect to see the current exchange rate between your local fiat currency and the cost per bitcoin to be shown.

Enter the amount of fiat currency, such as US Dollars, that you would like to invest. Remember that you can invest any amount as you do not have to buy whole multiples of bitcoins.

Figure 12: Buying Bitcoins With Cash, Part 1

Cash exchange sites sometimes allow you to select a bank that you will use to make your cash deposit. If so, you can make that selection as well, opting for a bank near your work or your home.

You will also want to enter the address of the bitcoin wallet to receive your bitcoins. Once you have entered this information carefully, click on "Continue to Next Step" or a similar link.

For example, you can enter $200 as the amount to invest in bitcoins. At a price of $816 per bitcoin, and minus any cash exchange fees, you may receive approximately one-quarter of a bitcoin. These bitcoins will be deposited at the wallet address you then provide on the form.

Next, you will be presented with a request for your email address. You will likely not be required to enter personally identifying information, yet an email address allows the exchanger to contact you in the event of some problem occurring in the exchange. I recommend that you enter a valid email address.

Figure 13: Buying Bitcoins With Cash, Part 2

You will be presented with the final cost breakdown including a fee paid to the exchanger for taking your cash and buying bitcoins on your behalf. If you are ready to proceed, then click on "Buy Bitcoins" to complete the order.

The final steps will then be presented to you. This will include a reminder to deposit the agreed-upon cash to the selected bank, and information about how to confirm the transaction with the exchanger.

Cash exchangers will typically require that you to keep the cash deposit receipt that you will receive from the bank and to write an order number on the receipt. Make sure to deposit cash rather than transferring money from your account to the exchangers, as cash is usually required rather than an account funds transfer. This type of transaction is not the same as depositing cash and may delay your purchase.

Figure 14: Buying Bitcoins With Cash, Part 3

You will then need to take a photo of the receipt, typically with your smartphone, and email the photo to a designated email address at the exchanger. Once they receive the email confirmation, they will buy the bitcoins on your behalf and send them to your specific wallet address. This entire process can occur in a matter of hours or may take several days depending on the exchanger's policies and the timing of your order.

RECEIVING BITCOINS

Another option to fund your wallet is for someone who already owns bitcoins to send you some. All you need to provide them with is your wallet address. Sending them an email with this address is the easiest way to get them the information they need.

I was helping a friend recently to get started with bitcoins and this is exactly what I did. Although the price of bitcoins was approaching $1,000 per bitcoin at the start of 2014, you don't need to give such a generous gift. You can simply send a fraction of a bitcoin worth a few dollars or even just a few cents.

I sent 0.0001 BTC, which at $816 per bitcoin was only about eight cents. This was a sufficient test to verify that I had the right bitcoin address and that my friend's wallet was working properly. This allowed my friend to practice copying and pasting her wallet address into an email message and sending it to me, and then for me to copy her wallet address into my wallet to send her the bitcoins. If we had made a mistake in our first transaction, very little would have been lost because of the error.

I will explain how to send bitcoins in the next chapter. Remember that it is good to have friends with bitcoins!

Marc A. Carignan

4

TRADING BITCOINS

WHAT IS TRADING?

Trading is simply buying or selling something of value. Similarly, trading bitcoins is the buying or selling of bitcoins. Trading bitcoins is quite similar to trading stocks online.

There is a current price per bitcoin as paired with most fiat currencies. Each bitcoin exchange displays the price at which buyers and sellers are currently trading bitcoins.

People who have used online stock trading will find bitcoin exchanges easy to use. Some newer bitcoin exchanges are even incorporating advanced stock purchase capabilities such as stop and limit orders. Although the fundamentals of stock trading are beyond the scope of this book, I will provide all you need to know to sell bitcoins on an exchange. Note that we already covered buying bitcoins in the last chapter in order to initially fund your wallet.

I will also explain how to send bitcoins, whether to someone else or to another bitcoin wallet that you own. These are basic operations that every bitcoin user needs to know.

WHAT IS AN EXCHANGE?

Exchanges are online sites that allow buyers and sellers to trade bitcoins. It is a marketplace where buyers and sellers come together to either buy or sell their bitcoins in exchange for something else of value, hence the name "exchange." Most online wallets are also exchanges as well, as I discussed earlier.

You don't need an exchange to simply send bitcoins to someone, yet if you want to exchange bitcoins for fiat currencies, you will need to find an exchange that works with your desired fiat. I have provided a listing of several such exchanges in the previous chapter.

CRYPTO EXCHANGES

A growing number of bitcoin exchanges allow you to trade other cryptocurrencies in addition to bitcoins. These crypto exchanges allow you to exchanging bitcoins for other cryptos, and if desired, back to bitcoins. I'll discuss the world of cryptos in more detail in a later chapter.

Here are some of the more popular crypto exchanges available today. Note that these exchanges may be located anywhere in the world as cryptos are truly global currencies:

- BTC-E (btc-e.com)

- Coins-E (coins-e.com)
- CoinEX (coinex.com)
- Cryptsy (cryptsy.com)
- mcxNOW (mcxnow.com)

Many of these crypto exchanges do not allow fiat currency exchanges at all. These exchanges expect you to you acquire your bitcoins or other cryptos elsewhere and transfer them into your wallet held at the crypto exchange, which also provides online wallet capabilities.

Transferring bitcoins from a fiat-to-crypto exchange like Coinbase to a crypto-to-crypto exchange like Cryptsy, for example, is easy. The process of transferring bitcoins to someone else or to one of your own wallets is identical.

It is important to note that bitcoins can only be sent to bitcoin wallets. Each different cryptocurrency has its own wallet address and its own public ledger, most often variations of the same blockchain concept at Bitcoin.

Some of the most popular cryptos include bitcoins, litecoins and peercoins. As cryptos can only be sent to wallets of their type, litecoins can only be sent to litecoin wallets and peercoins to peercoin wallets.

MANAGING YOUR CRYPTFOLIO

Sites like Cryptsy allow you to hold and trade multiple cryptocurrencies, transferring these cryptos into or out of your Cryptsy wallets. Each crypto requires its own crypto-specific wallet address, as I mentioned above. Although wallet addresses are different for each crypto, Cryptsy, for example, consolidates all the cryptos you own in a simple, easy-to-read crypto balances page. This makes the process of managing your cryptocurrency portfolio, or "cryptfolio," as simple as managing a list of stocks you may own.

You can decide if and when to "cash out" some of your cryptos into fiat currencies, even from crypto-to-crypto exchanges. Simply send the cryptos you wish to cash out to a wallet that allows the exchange of cryptos for fiat. For example, as Coinbase allows bitcoins and US Dollars to be exchanged, you can send bitcoins from Cryptsy to your Coinbase wallet if you want to sell them for dollars.

You may need to exchange cryptos like litecoins and peercoins back into bitcoins before cashing out to fiat, however. This is easy to do at a site like Cryptsy, where you can exchange a certain number of litecoins for bitcoins, and then send them to Coinbase to cash out. In this case, Coinbase allows cashing out to US Dollars, but only from bitcoins and not other cryptos. Watch for more flexibility among exchanges in the months ahead.

HOW TO SEND BITCOINS

Sending bitcoins is a common activity and is very easy to do. You need the bitcoin wallet address of the wallet to which you want to send the bitcoins. This address can be for your own wallet held in a different location or for someone else's wallet. You will, of course, also need to determine the amount of bitcoins to send.

Most online wallets provide an option called "Send" allowing you to transfer bitcoins out of your wallet and into another wallet elsewhere. Note that some online wallet sites call this feature "Withdraw" instead. Whatever the term used by your wallet, the feature works in the same way.

Fractional amounts of bitcoins are commonly used, such as 0.25 BTC for one-quarter of a bitcoin or 0.10 BTC for one-tenth of a bitcoin. There is no need to send whole bitcoins unless that is your intent.

You may optionally include a message that will be sent to the receiver along with the bitcoins. Think of this as a brief email message that will accompany the bitcoins. This message will be transmitted through the Bitcoin network along with the bitcoins. This is a useful way to describe the purpose for sending the bitcoins whether they are being sent as a gift, as a payment for a specific product or service or for some other reason. You can simply leave the message field blank if you prefer.

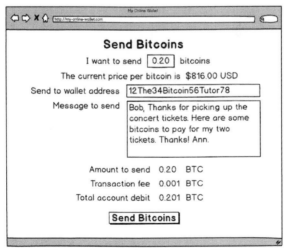

Figure 15: Sending Bitcoins Page

A small transaction fee of 0.001 BTC is typically paid for each transfer to encourage the Bitcoin network to process the transaction promptly. Officially, no fee is required, however, most online exchanges enforce a modest fee to reward the miners for this work. Note that at a bitcoin price of $816, this fee amounts to about 82 cents.

As I mentioned earlier, be sure to copy and paste the wallet addresses you use into your "Send Bitcoins" screen to prevent any errors that may occur by manually entering wallet addresses. This will ensure that you send your bitcoins to the right location.

SENDING BITCOINS TO A FRIEND

Sending bitcoins is the most important user activity in the Bitcoin network as bitcoins are always "pushed" to another and never "pulled." Therefore, every transaction in the Bitcoin network is a send, or push, transaction. Let's look at an example to make sure that this process is clear.

Let us say that Ann wants to transfer 0.20 bitcoins to her friend Bob to pay for upcoming concert tickets. The sequence of events would likely go something like this:

- Bob creates a new bitcoin wallet address in his online wallet or he can simply use an existing wallet address assigned to his wallet.
- Bob creates an email message asking Ann to transfer 0.20 BTC to his wallet, pastes his bitcoin wallet address into the email message and then sends the message.
- Ann receives the email message from Bob asking her to send him 0.20 BTC along with the wallet address that Bob would like Ann to use in sending the bitcoins.

- Ann opens her bitcoin wallet and clicks on the option to send bitcoins.

- Assuming she has at least 0.20 BTC in her wallet, she then clicks on the option to send bitcoins. If she doesn't have sufficient bitcoins, she will need to acquire some additional bitcoins as described previously.

- Ann copies the wallet address from Bob's email and pastes it into the "Send Bitcoins" screen in her online wallet as the destination wallet address.

- Ann then enters 0.20 BTC as the amount of bitcoins to send to Bob with a message saying that she is sending Bob the bitcoins in exchange for the concert tickets.

- Ann clicks the "Send Bitcoins" button to complete the transaction.

- Bob then receives the bitcoins shortly thereafter.

HOW TO RECEIVE BITCOINS

You may receive bitcoins anytime someone chooses to send them to your wallet. Providing the sender with your wallet address is all that is required. No specific action is needed to accept the bitcoins. Your wallet does not need to be open and your computer does not need to be turned on.

All the accounting of the transfer occurs in the blockchain and is reflected in your wallet the next time you connect.

HOW TO SELL BITCOINS

Bitcoins can be sold for various reasons. You may want to exchange them for a fiat currency, for another cryptocurrency or in exchange for goods or services.

Selling bitcoins is similar to selling stocks online. Prices vary from minute to minute based on what buyers and sellers are willing to negotiate on the various exchanges. Think of a screaming stock trader on a New York trading floor. There are those trying to buy and those trying to sell. They are shouting out their orders looking to buy or sell at a price that suits them and their clients best.

Bitcoin exchanges bring buyers and sellers together, although more quietly in an online exchange. Each exchange displays its current buy and sell prices for bitcoins and other currencies. These are called currency pairs. Buyers and sellers simply select the currency pair they want to trade, such as bitcoins for dollars, by clicking on the pair they want.

Cryptocurrency pairs are expressed with the currencies' three-letter codes, such as BTC/USD, BTC/EUR or BTC/LTC. These pairs refer to the price of bitcoins against US Dollars, bitcoins against euros and bitcoins against litecoins, respectively. Forex, or foreign currency exchange, trades are very similar in representing prices as currency pairs, except they provide this service only between fiat currencies rather than fiats and cryptos.

For each currency pair, the first currency listed is the crypto or fiat the trader chooses to trade. The second currency is the currency they will use to satisfy the trade. The currency pair BTC/USD, for example, expresses that bitcoins will be traded. If bitcoins are sold, US Dollars will be provided in exchange. If bitcoins are bought, US Dollars will be required to complete the trade.

Bitcoin and other crypto exchanges do not always allow trading between fiats and cryptos. Some exchanges trade exclusively between various cryptocurrencies.

CASHING OUT TO FIAT

Exchanges like Coinbase and Kraken allow you to buy bitcoins using fiat currencies and to sell bitcoins for fiats. This is the easiest way for people to "get in" or "get out" of cryptos like bitcoins and get back to their favorite fiat currencies.

Remember that any amount may be traded. Whole bitcoin amounts are not required. Fractional amounts like a half or a quarter of a bitcoin, written as 0.5 BTC or 0.25 BTC, respectively, may be easily bought and sold.

Figure 16: Selling Bitcoins For Deposit To A Bank Account

When selling bitcoins for fiats to be deposited directly into a linked bank account, you will need to specify the amount of bitcoins to sell and identify the bank account to receive the fiats. The bank account must be yours and must already be linked with your bitcoin wallet. Within a few days, your funds will appear in your bank.

CASHING OUT WITH PLASTIC

Another way to cash out is to use one of the new bitcoin debit cards. BitPlastic (bitplastic.com) is a company that provides a debit card and a corresponding online bitcoin wallet. You simply transfer your bitcoins to your BitPlastic wallet to fund your card. The card may then be used as any other debit card, allowing you to buy goods and services at point-of-sale businesses. You can also withdraw cash at traditional bank Automated Teller Machines (ATM's) with this card.

The current BTC/USD exchange rate, as managed by the BitPlastic exchange site, is automatically applied allowing you to easily exchange your bitcoins for use as US Dollars.

The Bitcoin Tutor does not endorse or recommend any specific wallet or exchange providers. The choice is yours to make.

CASHING OUT AT ATM's

The first bitcoin ATM's were introduced in 2013 by the company Robocoin (robocoinkiosk.com). The first one was installed in a Vancouver coffee shop and processed over 1 million Canadian Dollars (CAD) in its first month. These machines allow both the purchase of bitcoins with local fiat currency and the sale of bitcoins for fiat.

New bitcoin ATM's are planned for installation in the United States, Australia and Europe in 2014. This will provide another way to buy or sell bitcoins in person for people around the world.

CASHING OUT TO GOLD

Not everyone wants fiat currency. Many are choosing precious metals like gold and silver for their investments. At least one website now provides a direct exchange between bitcoins and gold. The site is called Coinabul (coinabul.com).

This site allows you to bypass exchanging bitcoins to fiat as an intermediate exchange, and then exchanging that fiat currency for precious metals. It provides a direct exchange to and from bitcoins and gold. It also offers a silver exchange for those who prefer to exchange bitcoins for silver rather than for gold.

You can expect to see many new ways to cash out your bitcoins and other cryptos in the months ahead.

SECURITY IS YOUR RESPONSIBILITY

Personal responsibility is of paramount importance in trading and managing cryptos like bitcoins. The security of your usernames, passwords and wallet addresses are your responsibility. There is no bank to complain to if you send the wrong person some bitcoins. There is no central authority to mediate.

Bitcoins are digital cash. Once you hand someone your cash, or bitcoins, it is now theirs unless they choose to return it.

How do you take responsibility? I recommend that you start by recording your wallet information, including your passwords, and storing them safely. You may write them down and keep them in a fireproof safe in your home. You may also record them in a computer-based password vault if you choose. Note that password vault discussions are beyond the scope of this book.

Another basic security step is to sign off, sometimes called logging off, from your online bitcoin wallets when you are done trading. Also, do not leave your computer unattended with your wallet open.

I recommend using common sense and comparing your bitcoin wallet to your physical one. Would you leave your physical wallet open with cash falling out of it at your favorite store and walk away? Would you expect everything to remain safe in your wallet if you did? I think not.

Another suggestion is to make sure someone you trust knows how to access your wallets once you have a level of significant ownership. You don't have to give them all the passwords directly, yet you can instruct them on how to retrieve them from your safe or other hiding place in the event of your incapacitation.

They will need to know which online sites you have selected to hold your bitcoins, your usernames and your passwords. Many people have acquired significant holdings in bitcoins and have either died or been incapacitated, unable to pass this wealth onto their heirs. Banks, lawyers, courts and other authorities or agencies cannot help your heirs if you do not provide this information. Even non-computer experts can access your holding with some assistance if they have the basic information.

Another security consideration is to start slowly when trading in bitcoins. Start with small amounts of money. If you lose $20, for example, it may be unfortunate but you won't have to sell your house. Starting slowly with smaller amounts of money allows you to build experience and confidence before moving on to larger transactions.

TWO-FACTOR AUTHENTICATION

My final suggestion is to increase your online wallet login security. This can be done with two-factor authentication. This additional security measure adds a significant level of difficulty for thieves who might try to break into your wallet, protecting your bitcoins from unauthorized access.

Wallets secured with two-factor security require more than your username and password. They require what is known as a "second factor."

Second factors vary across different online wallet providers. The most commonly used second factors today are provided as one-time passwords delivered by Short Message Service (SMS), otherwise known as mobile text messaging, or by using one-time password (OTP) generators. Wallets like Coinbase and Cryptsy, for example, allow you to setup two-factor security within their systems to better protect your wallet and its cryptocurrency contents.

SMS AS THE SECOND FACTOR

Second factor security using SMS requires that you register a mobile phone number to be associated with the online wallet. Make sure that your mobile phone accepts text messages. Once enabled, future logins will require an extra password that will be provided each time you login by text messages that will be sent to your mobile phone.

Figure 17: Two-Factor Authorization Setup Using SMS

Follow the steps to verify and activate SMS as a second factor. A test password will be send to your phone as part of this verification procedure. Once confirmed, you will need your phone every time you want to access your online wallet.

ONE-TIME PASSWORD GENERATORS

One-time password generators are computer applications available online or on mobile devices including iPhones, iPads and Android devices. These applications, known simply as "apps," are small programs that can be installed on your mobile devices to provide a second factor security without the need for SMS. This is particularly valuable if you are traveling internationally or out-of-range of traditional SMS messaging, since these apps typically do not require internet access to generate OTP's.

Two popular apps are Authy (authy.com) and Google Authenticator (google.com). Either or both of these apps may be used to generate the second passwords needed during login.

One-time password apps work by algorithmically generating OTP's, or one-time passwords, based on a specific "seed." This seed is a code that the wallet provider will display when setting up your wallet initially for two-factor authentication.

SETTING UP AN OTP GENERATOR

Here is the sequence you would use to enable two-factor authentication with the Google Authenticator app on your smartphone. Note that the app for Authy works in a similar way.

Login to your online wallet, click on "Account," "Security" or a similar link in your wallet, and select two-factor authentication. You may also need to select Google Authenticator as your preferred authentication app.

The online wallet site will generate a unique alphanumeric code and a corresponding QR Code.

Figure 18: Two-Factor Authorization Setup Using Google Authenticator

Open the Google Authenticator app on your smartphone. Select the option to add a new site authentication by tapping on a "+" sign or on a button named "Add" in the app.

Select the option to scan the QR Code automatically and then scan the code on the screen. Once scanned by Google Authenticator, an entry will be created in the app that will create a new six-digit OTP every 30 seconds based on the unique code, the "seed," initially provided.

Note that this app can manage multiple authentication codes, one for each of the wallets you may have.

Other authentication apps like Authy work in a very similar way. The length of the codes and the time provided to enter the codes may be different, however, from app to app. For example, Authy provides seven-digit OTP's and allows you 20 seconds to type them in.

Make sure to keep a copy of this original seed code for each wallet. You will need this code in the event that you change or lose your mobile phone. I recommend saving or printing a copy of the QR Code and the seed code, as just scanned by the Google Authenticator app. Store it in a safe along with your wallet usernames and passwords. With this kind of security, you don't want to lock yourself out of your own wallet.

Using An OTP Generator

Now that you have setup the one-time password generator, let us look at how to use it. Simply put, this generator will provide a secondary password that only someone with your phone will have access to. It is a secondary password that will change every 20-30 seconds and will be required after you enter your username and password each time you login.

Once two-factor authorization is enabled for your account, your login sequence will work something like this.

First, enter the web address for your wallet provider into your web browser and press enter. Once at the site, enter your username and password, as always, and click on "Sign In" or a similar button.

Figure 19: Wallet Sign-In With Username & Password

Rather than providing you with immediate access to your wallet as in the past, you will be presented with a second login screen. This second login will require you to use your Google Authenticator app to generate and then enter the proper secondary password.

Launch the app on your smartphone and find the entry for this particular wallet. Note that you may have secondary passwords for multiple wallets so be sure to select the right one.

Each OTP entry will be labeled with the name of the associated wallet in your app.

Read and then enter the one-time password on this screen. Note that each password that is generated will be valid for only 20-30 seconds so once you read the password, you will need to enter it without further delay. If you miss the timeline, don't worry. A new password is generated every 20-30 seconds. Just try it again.

Figure 20: Wallet Sign-In With A One-Time Password Generated By Google Authenticator

Other methods to add two-factor authentication continue to evolve, including using special devices that provide OTP's directly to the computer. In this case, you cannot login to your wallet without this special device.

Consider these options and remember to take responsibility and to save your passwords and OTP seed codes. Print these codes and store them in a safe location.

As as you are first starting out, take your time and be patient. You are on the cutting edge of a new revolution and the "edges" of this technology have not yet been all smoothed out.

Marc A. Carignan

5

USING BITCOINS

BUYING ONLINE WITH BITCOINS

Bitcoins are accepted at thousands of businesses worldwide including online and brick-and-mortar businesses, that is, businesses with physical stores. Bitcoins allow for payment of goods and services of all kinds.

Online bitcoin transactions appear to work very much like credit card transactions. You select the products you want to purchase, put them into an online shopping cart and then click on the checkout button. Based on the current bitcoin exchange rate with your local fiat currency, you will be provided a final price in bitcoins at checkout.

Merchants still source their goods and services in fiat currencies. Although bitcoins are accepted for payment, items are typically priced in fiat and converted to bitcoins at the time of purchase. For example, if the item total is $81.60 then 0.1 BTC may be the bitcoin purchase price.

Click to make your purchase if you accept the bitcoin price that is presented. You will be asked for an email address so that the merchant can communicate with you. A shipping address will be required as well if you are buying a physical product, yet will not be required if your goods are digital such as music or information downloads. This provides an additional level of identity security in your transactions, a significant improvement in your personal privacy over credit and debit card transactions today, which require identity disclosure for every online transaction.

A merchant wallet address will be displayed along with a QR Code once you accept the option to purchase with bitcoins. You will be provided about 10 minutes to complete the transaction by transferring the stated number of bitcoins from your desired wallet to the merchant. Mobile wallet apps can simply scan the QR Code for the fastest payment options. Simply scan, enter the amount to pay and click Send on your mobile device.

Paying from an online wallet is easy as well. Simply login to your online wallet in another browser window, click on the option to send bitcoins and enter the amount of bitcoins to send. Copy the merchant wallet address and paste it into your wallet screen to send bitcoins to the merchant. Make sure that you copied and pasted the address correctly before clicking to send the bitcoins.

You will then receive an email confirmation from the merchant within a few minutes to confirm the transaction. Note that it will take an hour or two for the merchant to confirm receipt of the bitcoins.

Congratulations. You have now purchased something online with bitcoins!

ONLINE SITES THAT ACCEPT BITCOINS

There are a growing number of online sites that accept bitcoins. Here are a few of the online stores available today that accept bitcoins as payment for electronics, gardening supplies, gift cards, gold and silver, health products, music downloads, online gambling, prescription drugs, sporting goods and more. Many of these sites also accept fiat currencies, such as dollars or euros, as payment, and some are strictly bitcoin merchants:

- BitRoad (bitroad.co.uk)
- BitcoinShop (bitcoinshop.us)
- BitcoinStore (bitcoinstore.com)
- CheapAir (cheapair.com)
- Coinabul (coinabul.com)
- CoinRx (coinrx.com)
- Gyft (gyft.com/bitcoin)
- NameCheap (namecheap.com)
- Overstock (overstock.com)
- Pirate Bay, The (thepiratebay.se)
- Pizza For Coins (pizzaforcoins.com)
- Reddit (reddit.com)
- Tesla Motors (teslamotors.com)
- Tiger Direct (tigerdirect.com)
- Virgin Galactic (virgingalactic.com)
- Wordpress (wordpress.com)
- Zynga (zynga.com)

In addition, a growing number of universities are accepting tuition payments in bitcoins:

- Draper University (draperuniversity.com)
- University of Cumbria (cumbria.ac.uk)
- University of Nicosia (unic.ac.cy)

Investment firms dedicated to Bitcoin company investments include the following companies:

- Andreesen Horowitz (a16z.com)
- Bit Angels (bitangels.co)
- Seedcoin (seedco.in)

The links above are subject to change yet the businesses that accept bitcoins will only continue to grow. Note that I have not done business with all these vendors so I will leave it up to you to determine which businesses that you may find the most interesting and valuable.

BUYING IN PERSON WITH BITCOINS

You may use bitcoins at thousands of brick-and-mortar, or physical stores, throughout the world. There are enclaves where bitcoins are really taking off, including in San Francisco, California and Berlin, Germany. In-person purchases, whether with credit cards or with bitcoins, are often referred to as point-of-sale (POS) transactions.

A mobile wallet is needed to transact bitcoins in person. Whether paying your bill in a bar, a coffee shop or a grocery store, the process is the same.

Merchants need to provide their wallet address for you to use in sending them bitcoins. The address will be provided as a QR Code for you to scan with your mobile wallet app. Scanning this code prevents the problems that might arise if you had to type in a wallet address by hand into your mobile phone.

Scanning the QR Code with your bitcoin mobile wallet app will bring up a mobile screen that allows you to review and approve the charge. You will be able to enter the total in bitcoins, or in some cases, the QR Code you scan will already have the price included. In the case of restaurants and bars, you will also be able to add a tip or gratuity in bitcoins as well. Review the bill, enter any changes, and tap on the button to complete the transaction.

The merchant will be notified of your transaction within seconds, in about as fast as it takes to receive an email message. Funds will be available to the merchant in as little as an hour, following transaction confirmations within the Bitcoin network. Merchants may also setup their wallet to automatically convert the bitcoins received into local fiat currency eliminating exposure to the price fluctuations of bitcoins. Universities and larger retailers often choose this automatic conversion option, from bitcoins into fiat, to eliminate the financial risks associated with the current price fluctuations of bitcoin.

Note that you can use your bitcoin wallet to pay people directly, and not simply to pay established vendors as is the case today with credit cards. Try paying your babysitter with a credit card. Unless you have hired a professional agency, the neighbor next door probably does not accept Visa or Mastercard. Yet, they can accept bitcoins.

Bitcoin, on the other hand, allows you to transfer payment to anyone at any time. No special merchant accounts are required. Whether it's a family member, a friend or the babysitter, just copy and paste their wallet address into your wallet or scan their personal QR Code directly from their smartphone. Enter the amount of bitcoins to send and click the button on your computer, or tap it on your smartphone, to send the bitcoins.

BUSINESSES THAT ACCEPT BITCOINS IN PERSON

The number of businesses accepting bitcoins and other cryptos in person is growing rapidly. Businesses around the world are now accepting bitcoins. The website CoinMap (coinmap.org) provides a worldwide map that locates many of the businesses that accept bitcoins today, whether you are in North America, Europe or Asia. Another way to find businesses that accept bitcoins is to visit the website SpendBitcoins (spendbitcoins.com).

Merchants who want to accept bitcoins online or in-person should visit two popular merchant wallet companies, BitPay (bitpay.com) and Coinbase (coinbase.com). These companies provide everything you need to accept bitcoins at your business.

OTHER WAYS TO USE BITCOINS

Coinbase and a growing number of other companies allow their employees to be paid in bitcoins. A police chief in Kentucky made headlines in 2013 when he requested to be paid in bitcoins, a request that the city commission approved.

Wages paid in bitcoins are currently calculated in local fiat, such as US Dollars, and converted to bitcoins at the current exchange rate. All applicable local and national taxes are paid in fiat and deducted prior to conversion, of course. After all, fiats are the governments' money and is how they expect to be paid.

A United States Congressman also started accepting bitcoins for campaign contributions in 2013. You can expect to see many new examples of bitcoin acceptance in the months and years ahead.

SENDING OTHER CRYPTOS

Cryptocurrencies other than bitcoins work in similar ways. Not all cryptos have mobile wallets at this time. All cryptos, however, have online wallets that make it easy to send and receive these currencies.

It is important to note that wallet addresses are specific to each cryptocurrency. Your bitcoin address will not allow you to receive litecoins, for example. You would need your litecoin address.

Online wallets that support many cryptos provide a method to access each crypto-specific wallet address allowing you to provide the right address for the right crypto. These wallets allow you to see all of your crypto holdings in a single view. This unified view of all of your crypto holdings is known as your cryptfolio.

Marc A. Carignan

6

ALTERNATIVE CRYPTOS

HUNDREDS OF ALTCOINS

There are well over 200 cryptocurrencies trading today, most of which are derivatives of the Bitcoin protocol. Each crypto has its own unique twist on Bitcoin, and in the last example below, was created independently of Bitcoin. Alternative cryptos are often called "altcoins," short for alternative coins, as they are considered alternatives to bitcoins.

It is unlikely that all of these altcoins will gain mass appeal. It seems, however, that there will be uses for several of these cryptos as most altcoins focus on some unique aspect of Bitcoin that their creators believe improve upon the Bitcoin approach.

I will present several cryptos below beginning with Bitcoin. These cryptos are typically traded in pairs with bitcoins or litecoins, which are among the cryptocurrencies most frequently used today in crypto trading.

Sites like Cryptsy allow trading between over a hundred crypto pairs, such as BTC/LTC (bitcoin/litecoin), PPC/BTC (peercoin/bitcoin) and QRK/LTC (quark/litecoin). There is no guarantee that all of these cryptocurrencies will be successful, yet they are some of the more popular cryptos that I find interesting and that I believe are worth watching.

BITCOIN

It all starts with Bitcoin (BTC). Key benefits of Bitcoin include:

- Transactions occur almost instantly in the peer-to-peer Bitcoin network.
- Zero or very low processing fees are incurred in trading bitcoins.
- A secure hashing algorithm, SHA-256, is used to cryptographically secure bitcoin transactions. SHA-256 was developed by the NSA and is considered virtually unbreakable.
- Open source software is used to prevent the Bitcoin protocol from being corrupted or rigged by criminals. It allows a large community of developers to support and, over time, improve the Bitcoin network.
- As per its original design, a maximum of 21 million bitcoins will be mined, allowing the crypto to remain scarce, a feature of all true money.
- A new block of coins is mined every 10 minutes and added to the blockchain.

- All coins are expected to be mined by 2040.

Altcoins are nearly always compared to the perceived or actual limitations of Bitcoin. Here are some of the concerns with Bitcoin that altcoins typically try to address:

- Specialized computer hardware is now required to mine bitcoins due to computational difficulty imposed by the network, as per design.

- Mining is relatively expensive as it is estimated to cost over $150,000 per day for all bitcoin miners in existence today. This is not seen as a reason to abandon Bitcoin, yet rather a barrier to entry for criminals as well as for small computer miners.

- Clearing transactions takes longer than the ideal for widespread usage as verification requires 60 minutes on the Bitcoin network, which are six confirmation intervals of 10 minutes each. Although much faster than credit cards and wire transfers, bitcoin transactions are still slower than in-person cash transactions that are final when the cash changes hands. This is an area that altcoins often improve upon.

- Scaling the network to many millions of transactions per day is seen as a concern. This is an area that the Bitcoin developers continue to research and will likely enhance in the years ahead.

Based on the bitcoin opening price on January 1, 2014, 1 BTC was valued at $816.00. Put another way, 1 USD could purchase 0.00122549 BTC, or just over 0.1% of a bitcoin. Visit bitcoin.org for more information.

LITECOIN

If Bitcoin is the new gold, then Litecoin (LTC) is the new silver. Based on the Bitcoin protocol, its benefits include:

- Litecoins can be mined efficiently with consumer-grade computer hardware versus specialized, high-end, expensive hardware as required for bitcoin mining.

- Rather than using the SHA-256 cryptographic algorithm as in Bitcoin, Litecoin uses the Scrypt algorithm, which defines the computationally intensive work that Litecoin performs to generate each new block. This algorithm was specifically designed to make it costly to perform computer hardware attacks by requiring large amounts of memory to do so. Several other altcoins now use Scrypt as well.

- Transaction confirmations occur at 2.5-minute intervals for Litecoin versus 10-minute intervals for Bitcoin.

- A greater number of litecoins than bitcoins will be mined, up to 84 million in total.

- Litecoins are currently worth substantially less than bitcoins. This has the psychological advantage of allowing people to own tens or hundreds of litecoins as opposed to only a few bitcoins for the same investment.

Based on the bitcoin opening price on January 1, 2014, 1 BTC was roughly equivalent in value to 30 LTC; at $816.00 per bitcoin, 1 LTC was valued at $27.20. Put another way, 1 USD could purchase 0.03676471 LTC, or about 4% of a litecoin. Visit litecoin.org for more information.

PEERCOIN

Peercoin (PPC) is also based on the Bitcoin protocol. It bills itself as a green coin as it is considered more sustainable to mine and transact than many other cryptos. Benefits include:

- The Peercoin network consumes far less energy in its mining process due to its more efficient hashing function.

- The network maintains stronger security due to an algorithmic improvement over Bitcoin, something called proof-of-stake versus proof-of-work. Peercoin, in fact, implements a hybrid approach which puts any attacker at a greater risk of losing their own wealth than the wealth they would be trying to acquire from others.

- There is no hard limit on the number of peercoins that can be created. It is designed, however, to eventually achieve a 1% inflation rate, limiting the amount of new coins created per year. This approach is intended to increase supply to meet demand yet provide sufficient scarcity to maintain the value of peercoins.

Based on the bitcoin opening price on January 1, 2014, 1 BTC was roughly equivalent in value to 150 PPC; at $816.00 per bitcoin, 1 PPC was valued at $5.44. Put another way, 1 USD could purchase 0.18382353 PPC, or about 18% of a peercoin. Visit peercoin.net for more information.

QUARK

Quark (QRK), sometimes referred to as Quarkcoin, is another Bitcoin protocol derivative. Its benefits include:

- Improved security using nine rounds of secure hashing from six different algorithms allows more secure transaction processing than a single hashing algorithm, as most cryptos use. Although a single hash function today is considered sufficient, the Quark developers wanted to provide additional layers of security against future unknowns.

- The number of new quarks being mined is substantially less than other coins as the majority of the coins were premined. This approach is anticipated to reduce the price volatility of quarks as opposed to other cryptos due to a lower rate of dilution as is usually created by the mining of new coins.

- The mining and transaction confirmation process takes only 30 seconds to complete.

- A total of about 247 million quarks will be mined by early 2014, and then about 1 million additional coins will be mined per year afterwards.

Based on the bitcoin opening price on January 1, 2014, 1 BTC was roughly equivalent in value to 6,500 QRK; at $816.00 per bitcoin, 1 QRK was valued at $0.12, or 12 cents. Put another way, 1 USD could purchase 8.33333333 QRK, or just over 8 quarks. Visit qrk.cc for more information.

MEGACOIN

Megacoin (MEC) is also a derivative of Bitcoin. Benefits of Megacoin include:

- Only 42 million megacoins will be mined of which half are already currently in circulation.

- Transactions take only seconds to process and confirmations occur every two and a half minutes.
- Although not yet implemented, Megacoin has the ability to implement true anonymous transactions versus what are known today as pseudonymous transactions as with most other cryptos today including bitcoins.

Based on the bitcoin opening price on January 1, 2014, 1 BTC was roughly equivalent in value to 850 MEC; at $816.00 per bitcoin, 1 MEC was valued at $0.96, or 96 cents. Put another way, 1 USD could purchase 1.04166667 MEC, or just over 1 megacoin. Visit megacoin.co.nz for more information.

ZETACOIN

Zetacoin (ZET), based on Bitcoin, has benefits that include:

- Zetacoin features fast transaction times and fast mining difficulty adjustments, making the mining process simpler.
- A total of 160 million coins will be initially mined of which nearly all have been mined.
- A yearly inflation amount of 1 million coins will be mined thereafter.

Based on the bitcoin opening price on January 1, 2014, 1 BTC was roughly equivalent in value to 17,000 ZET; at $816.00 per bitcoin, 1 ZET was valued at $0.048, or 4.8 cents. Put another way, 1 USD could purchase 20.83333333 ZET, or almost 21 zetacoins. Visit zeta-coin.org for more information.

MAXCOIN

Maxcoin (MAX), one of the newest cryptocurrencies based on the Bitcoin protocol, has the backing of popular talk show host Max Keiser, for whom the coin is named. Max and his wife, Stacy Herbert, co-host the popular international financial television show, the "Keiser Report" (maxkeiser.com).

Its benefits include:

- Maxcoin uses a newer cryptographic algorithm known as Keccak, pronounced as "ketch-ack", an SHA-3 cryptographic function. This is currently a CPU-minable coin versus a GPU or ASIC hardware minable coin, as most other cryptos employ. This means that regular computers without specialized hardware can mine this coin.

- A total of 250 million coins will be mined of which none were premined, creating a "fair launch" of this new crypto, without concern of early developers having lined their pockets with pre-generated coins.

- Miners receive 96 maxcoins per block, with the reward per block halving approximately every 12 months.

- Mining difficulty is retargeted using the advanced Kimoto Gravity Well algorithm.

- And, blocks are created every 30 seconds, accelerating transaction and confirmation times.

Maxcoin launched on February 5, 2014. Only ten days later, maxcoin was already considered the 18th most valuable crypto in the world according to Crypto-Currency Market Capitalizations (coinmarketcap.com), with a total market capitalization of over $3.7 million US Dollars.

At its February 15, 2014 price of $2.45 per maxcoin, it is off to a tremendous start as a new altcoin. Based on the current price of bitcoin, at $649.00, 1 BTC is roughly equivalent in value to 264.90 MAX. Put another way, 1 USD could purchase 0.40816327 MAX, or about 40% of a single maxcoin.

Yes, maxcoins are already more valuable that the US Dollar! Visit maxcoin.co.uk for more information.

MAZACOIN

Mazacoin (MZC) is the first cryptocurrency to be created to serve as a national currency. The Oglala Lakota Nation, a Native American tribe, is part of the Sioux Nation whose land spans the western half of the US State of South Dakota. They have publicly adopted mazacoin as their new national currency, a decision that will replace the United States Dollar as its preferred currency.

Its developers have designed the coin to have a minimum useful lifespan of at least a century, according to their website. It has been specifically designed to mimic the value and rarity of precious metals and to include anti-deflationary measures. They believe that these elements will ensure the value stability of mazacoins for the purpose of wealth storage.

A total of 2.4192 billion coins will be mined in the first 5 years with a yearly inflation amount of 1 million coins to be added thereafter. Blocks are created every two minutes for speedy transactions with five confirmations needed. That is, all transactions can be confirmed in as little as 10 minutes, releasing the funds to the receiver of the mazacoins.

Mazacoin launched in late February 2014. By March 8, 2014, mazacoin was trading at $0.017, or just under two cents per mazacoin, with a total market cap of over $208,000 US Dollars. Visit mazacoin.org for more information.

AURORACOIN

Auroracoin (AUC) is being developed as a cryptocurrency for Iceland.

Five years ago, the financial system of Iceland collapsed and the government imposed capital controls, which are still in place today. This has limited business people from exchanging Iceland Kronas (ISK) to other fiat currencies such as US Dollars and Euros. International investment has diminished, as foreigners cannot risk being unable to convert their krona investments back into their national currencies.

An Icelandic developer, Baldur Friggjar Odinsson, is developing this alternative to the krona for use within Iceland and for exchange around the world. Odinsson is planning an "airdrop," that is, he plans to give every citizen of Iceland an initial allocation of auroracoins to encourage them to begin using the currency. Each citizen is slated to receive 31.8 AUC based on having their Iceland national ID number available to verify their identities.

Auroracoin is based on Litecoin and is 50% premined. Other developers are being encouraged to participate and create tools for Auroracoin to support its adoption as well.

Auroracoin launched in late February 2014. By March 8, 2014, auroracoin was trading at an amazing $26.93, with a total market cap of over $435,000 US Dollars. Visit auroracoin.org for more information.

RIPPLE

Ripple (XRP) is one of a few cryptocurrencies that is not based on the Bitcoin protocol. Ripple was created for a single purpose, that is, to facilitate the transfer of funds from one person to another worldwide.

As opposed to the cryptos described above, the Ripple network and the currency by the same name are separate. National fiat currencies, rather than the ripple currency, can be sent via the Ripple network. Ripple can provide this service for a fraction of the cost of traditional moneychangers today due to its efficient and secure implementation.

Ripple currency is used for two primary reasons. A small amount of ripples are purchased and transmitted with each transaction as a small transaction fee. This fee, however small, prevents network spam from being transmitted across the Ripple network, as each message requires a small payment. Imagine how much less email spam you would receive if every spammer had to pay 3 cents per email message. This small fee encourages only serious users of Ripple to participate.

A second reason to use ripples is as an exchange currency. This allows US Dollars, for example, to be exchanged for ripples for a brief time and later transmitted and exchanged to a destination currency, such as euros.

The benefits of Ripple include:

- The Ripple network is currency agnostic. It can transmit or exchange between any fiat currency pairs or between fiats and ripples.

- Transactions are recorded in a ledger on a distributed network, similar to Bitcoin's blockchain.

- Consensus is reached by the network every 2 to 5 seconds allowing for the rapid trading of assets and settlement of transactions.

- Payments clear in seconds because of the rapid consensus time.

Based on the bitcoin opening price on January 1, 2014, 1 BTC was roughly equivalent in value to 27,000 XRP; at $816.00 per bitcoin, 1 XRP was valued at $0.0302, or just over 3 cents. Put another way, 1 USD could purchase 33.11258278 XRP, or just over 33 ripples. Visit ripple.com for more information.

7

WHAT'S NEXT?

BITCOIN IS MORE THAN MONEY

I believe that Bitcoin is about far more than the digital equivalent of cash. It is about more than a decentralized public ledger of transactions and ownership. It is also about more than creating the world's largest decentralized supercomputer as well. In truth it is all these things, and more.

Bitcoin technology is likely to revolutionize digital money. It also has the possibility to change the way we buy and sell nearly everything. It can track ownership of assets from houses and cars to stock and bonds. It can track and prove the creation dates of original works of art, writing and inventions. It can include information within each transaction that includes contracts, articles, books, patents and copyrights. It can even store this information as open text or encrypted within the blockchain.

Bitcoin technology will also get easier to use. The dangers and risks will be mitigated. The problems will be resolved. The difficulties in managing personal wallet security will be simplified. The markets will grow. And, the acceptance of bitcoins will grow worldwide.

MAINFRAMES, PC'S & THE INTERNET

The computer industry has created fundamentally transforming technologies almost every decade. It started with a few, room-filling computers that cost millions of dollars and were limited to engineering, mathematical and financial applications requiring substantial computational power. Computers were expensive and limited to a select few. People who controlled and managed these systems required programming skills and creative thinking that was part science and part art.

Mainframes evolved from requiring punch cards for programming to utilizing computer terminals to access computers in real-time. This simplified the work of programming and managing these computers and ushered in thousands of professionals into Information Technology and Computer Science programs. Most people thought that the need for computers would never exceed a few hundred worldwide, including the leaders of some of the biggest computer companies of that time.

Luckily, a few visionaries saw it differently…

Mainframes opened the door to personal computers. These early PC's were clunky, slow and hard to use. They ran operating systems like DOS and CP/M. They provided a simple screen that required cryptic commands to use.

Then the Mac was born and DOS gave way to Windows, offering a graphical user interface rather than the old command line approach. Personal computers became a must-have in every business, school and home. Word processing, spreadsheets and accounting software became indispensable tools for nearly every business. Computers were now on every desktop or laptop. Many thought that this was great and perhaps the pinnacle of computer usefulness in our lives.

Luckily, a few visionaries saw it differently…

A branch of the United States' Department of Defense created the Advanced Research Projects Agency Network named ARPAnet. This system allowed the testing of new networking technologies, linking many universities and research centers. A new method of sharing information over this network called Hypertext Markup Language (HTML) was created and this network was then opened up to commercial interests, being renamed the Internet.

The early Internet days were challenging. HTML had to be written by hand. Email was unreliable as computers connected to or withdrew from the network at various times. However, the Internet became more resilient over time. HTML editing programs were created to simply the creation of websites. New tools and technologies improved the experiences of the Internet for publishers and users.

Internet browsers became standardized and were available on every computer. These browsers became more powerful and business was now possible online. Many saw this as a brave new world with opportunities to attract business across the world with this new power to buy and sell goods and services online. A new world of online commerce, or e-commerce, had been created. This was surely the final episode in the value of computers and technology.

Luckily, some visionaries saw it differently…

BITCOIN IS THE NEXT TRANSFORMATION

In 2008, following the disruption of the global financial markets, Satoshi Nakamoto had an idea. The problem of digital cash, private ownership and proof of that ownership was a computer problem that had yet to be solved. This was true despite the brightest minds having been focused on this problem for decades. A new concept was needed to bring the vision of digital cash to life. A method that would not require a central bank or governing authorities was sought.

A white paper entitled *Bitcoin: A Peer-to-Peer Electronic Cash System* was written and published by Satoshi Nakamoto. This technical paper described the Bitcoin concept and how it would solve a wide variety of challenges that would likely be encountered. The core problem plaguing proof of digital ownership, decentralization and processing transactions had been solved with a combination of cryptography and a unique proof-of-work scheme that was revolutionary in its approach.

Today, Bitcoin operates with thousands of miners across the globe that maintain the network. The network itself was

THE BITCOIN TUTOR

designed to create sufficient financial incentives to keep the decentralized system running. It also created a low financial barrier to entry for buyers and sellers who wanted to transact with each other with bitcoins.

Bitcoin's market capitalization was almost $10 billion on January 1, 2014 and many believe that the run in value has only begun. Yet, Bitcoin has its challenges today.

SOME BITCOIN CHALLENGES

There are several Bitcoin challenges to be addressed in the years ahead. It is relatively easy to lose bitcoins if you forget your password or lose your private key. Passing this wealth to heirs requires planning and preparation prior to incapacitation or death. Wallets and exchanges are inconsistent, having various levels of security and not utilizing naming conventions, which have yet to be created.

If Bitcoin follows the other trends that I discussed above, then you have the opportunity to "get in early" with bitcoins and other cryptocurrencies before bitcoins hit the mainstream. Bitcoin will get easier to use. It will get safer. Millions of people will learn about Bitcoin. And then, many of these people will enter the market with their interest and their dollars, causing price to rise and acceptance to grow even further.

Here you are today. You are learning about Bitcoin in the early days of this breakthrough technology. Where will this ride take you?

- Will you increase your bitcoin wealth by virtue of its growing popularity and usability?

- Will you buy stocks and bonds through a Bitcoin-based exchange rather than through traditional stockbrokers or online stock trading sites?
- Will you buy your next house with proof of ownership stored in the Bitcoin blockchain?
- Will your next original invention, book, song or artwork be copyrighted or patented with indelible proof stored and time-stamped in the blockchain?
- Will you be profiting from these changes, continuing to learn and investing in your own education? Or, will you be standing on the sidelines wondering how to get involved or perhaps wishing that you had invested earlier?

Bitcoin is the first true digital cash, yet it is not just about money. It is an entire programming environment for decentralized processing, tracking ownership and securing wealth. Its public leader, the blockchain, is itself a revolutionary concept. With the proof-of-work computations that are required to secure it, the blockchain is effectively impossible to corrupt.

REALIZING THE FUTURE VALUE

Each of these inventions, mainframes, PC's, the internet and Bitcoin, were not seen as the revolutionary and transforming technologies that they later became. Who would have expected to have billions of computers in the world, from mainframes to laptops to mobile devices? I have often said "there's more computing power in the doorknob of my hotel room today that there was in the space ships that took men to the moon!"

Realize that the future of many industries lies before you today in Bitcoin. This is a fundamentally disruptive technology that has the potential to change "everything."

How many people would have thought just a decade ago that many households would have or even want dozens of computers in their home? Personal computers, smartphones, tablets, music players, cable boxes, digital video recorders, game consoles, karaoke machines and other devices are all computers and their developments were generally unexpected by most people.

Today, looking back at the path that got us here, we see this development as inevitable. I believe that Bitcoin and its potential benefits are also inevitable.

CRYPTOCURRENCY INVESTMENT IS SPECULATIVE

We are in the early days of bitcoins and cryptocurrencies. No single group, government or agency is likely to prevent its growth. Some will, of course, try to stop or disrupt this movement. There will be those in power who will regulate, limit or otherwise redirect some efforts with cryptocurrencies. Some of these efforts may be positive; others may not. Yet this will not derail the power and momentum of Bitcoin.

Bitcoin is an investment and trading vehicle today in its function as a cryptocurrency. Be aware that all cryptos are speculative, highly volatile investments today. Nothing in this book has been intended to be investment advice for potential readers. I have done my best to explain the pros and cons, provide step-by-step instructions for using the Bitcoin technology and have offered ideas as to why Bitcoin may have a bright future.

The value of bitcoins really took off in 2013. Hundreds of new cryptos were also introduced that year. I expect to see more volatility in the months ahead, leading eventually to stable alternative currencies.

We are likely to see several of the cryptos emerge as leaders while others will fade away. News reports, both for and against bitcoins and other cryptocurrencies, will increase as more attention is placed on cryptos. Expect sometimes-shocking news and great developments as well.

FUTURE BITCOIN TRENDS

Here are some future trends that I see for bitcoins and other cryptocurrencies.

I expect to see many more merchants adopting bitcoins and other cryptos as an alternative form of payment. Some merchants are already offering discounts for customers who choose to pay in bitcoins versus fiat currencies, providing an incentive for people to pay using this new currency. Bitcoins are attractive to merchants as they can easily save 3% or more on transaction costs otherwise paid to banks and credit card processors.

Money transfers, from person to person locally and across the world, will become substantially cheaper. Companies such as Western Union may become the dinosaurs of the future unless they start using cryptos as a means of exchange and avoiding slow and expensive banks for money transmission. They will need to pass a substantial part of the savings on to their customers as well to compete in the near future.

Governments will meet to consider legal status, regulations and tax compliance policies for bitcoins and cryptos. Will bitcoins be considered currencies, securities, commodities or a class of their own? Only time will tell.

Even the United States Military is involved in Bitcoin. The US Air Force is reportedly building a Bitcoin payment gateway funded by a Small Business Innovation Research (SBIR) grant awarded to the Department of Defense.

THERE IS MORE TO LEARN

This purpose of this book was not to provide everything there is to know about Bitcoin. Bitcoin is new for everyone and you are now at the "top of the class" by having basic knowledge about Bitcoin, cryptocurrencies and the possibilities for their future.

Other areas that you may want to learn more may include:

- Beginner, intermediate and advanced learning programs
- Bitcoin arbitrage trading opportunities
- Cold storage, using various types of offline and paper wallets, for additional security
- Cryptocurrency trading strategies
- Researching blockchain transactions with block explorers
- Merchant step-by-step options to accept bitcoins or other cryptos
- Mining cryptos in solo, pool or cloud mining setups

- Tax guidelines and government regulations
- Wallet and transaction security techniques
- Trading and wallet step-by-step video learning series
- And, advanced uses of cryptos including escrow services, copyrights, patent filings, etc. that may occur in the future

Many of these programs will become available in the months ahead at our companion website for *The Bitcoin Tutor*, at thebitcointutor.com.

OTHER RESOURCES

Here are a few additional websites that provide valuable news and information about bitcoins and cryptocurrencies:

- Bitcoin Foundation (bitcoinfoundation.org)
- Bitcoin Magazine (bitcoinmagazine.com)
- Bitcoin VOX (bitcoinvox.com)
- BitcoinWisdom (bitcoinwisdom.com)
- BitLegal (bitlegal.net)
- CoinDesk (coindesk.com)
- Crypto-Currency Market Capitalizations (coinmarketcap.com)
- Keiser Report (maxkeiser.com)
- We Use Coins (weusecoins.com)

WE ARE MAKING HISTORY

By being part of Bitcoin today, we are making history. I fully believe that our children and their children will look back to this time in history as a pivotal time in human cultural and economic development. We are changing the world.

Welcome to the journey. Welcome to a part of history being created today!

Marc A. Carignan

LEARNING MORE

ASSISTING PEOPLE TO LEARN

The Bitcoin Tutor is dedicated to assisting people to learn about, use and profit from cryptocurrencies, the future of money. For those brave enough to lead into this new world, there will likely be handsome profits to be made. For those who love being at the front edge of something new, this is the place to be.

As many questions were not answered in this book, I have provided a free report, "The Bitcoin Tutor Strategies Report," for download from *The Bitcoin Tutor* website, at thebitcointutor.com. I invite you to visit this site and to continue learning about Bitcoin.

This website provides a free monthly newsletter with important information about the evolving world of Bitcoin.

Investors will want to know about new opportunities. Business people will want to profit from accepting bitcoins and other cryptos. And, everyone will benefit from the knowledge and savings that bitcoins can provide.

Check back at *The Bitcoin Tutor* website often as we continue launch additional learning opportunities from month to month, including new books, videos, action guides, training programs, webinars and more. The journey is only just beginning and *The Bitcoin Tutor* is dedicated to being the place for you to go to keep learning and to profit from your knowledge of Bitcoin and cryptocurrencies! We look forward to being your "tutor!"

CONNECTING WITH ME ONLINE

You can connect with me online at *The Bitcoin Tutor* (thebitcointutor.com). I am also on social media including Facebook and Twitter. Visit me on Facebook at facebook.com/TheBitcoinTutor or tweet me on Twitter at @TheBitcoinTutor. Follow me to stay in touch with the latest on Bitcoin and the future of your money.

Here's to your success, your education and your profits!

GLOSSARY

ALTCOINS

Altcoins refer to alternative coins, that is, cryptocurrencies that are alternatives to bitcoins. Altcoins are also referred to as cryptos, or cryptocurrencies.

BITCOIN

Bitcoin refers to the technology, the network and the currency. When referring to the technology or the network, the term is typically capitalized as Bitcoin; when referring to the currency, the term is typically written in lowercase at bitcoins. See further definitions below.

BITCOIN
*(THE TECHNOLOGY
AND THE NETWORK
OF BITCOIN)*

Bitcoin, the technology, is a peer-to-peer payment and information tracking system that is decentralized, uses cryptography to secure information and introduces an innovative proof-of-work system to securely process transactions. The Bitcoin network is operated by a decentralized group of computers, called miners that process bitcoin currency transactions. Bitcoin was introduced as open source software, or software that is free to use, by Satoshi Nakamoto in 2009.

BITCOIN
(BITCOIN AS A
CURRENCY)

Bitcoin is the first digital currency that was designed to prevent double spending. Bitcoins can be exchanged, person-to-person, without the need for a centralized authority or other third party. Bitcoins are the world's first cryptocurrency, a cryptographically secure digital currency. Bitcoins are processed on the Bitcoin network.

BLOCKCHAIN

The blockchain is a public ledger that is created, secured and maintained by miners within the Bitcoin network. It includes the history of all transactions, is cryptographically secured and requires consensus among the majority of miners in order for any changes to be committed to the ledger.

COMMODITIES

Commodities are items of value that require either human or mechanical labor to be mined, extracted, farmed, ranched or raised. Gold, oil, wheat, cattle and pork bellies are examples of commodities that are valued and traded worldwide.

COMMODITY-BASED CURRENCIES

Currencies that are backed by commodities, or items of intrinsic value, are commodity-based. Gold is most commonly used to back the value of a currency by maintaining a percentage of gold on reserve for each currency unit issued. These government-issued currencies generally require commodities to back at least 30% of the face value of the currency. This currency is often considered to be true money.

CRYPTFOLIO

Cryptfolio is a term used for a cryptocurrency portfolio. A cryptfolio is similar in nature to a stock portfolio, where various stocks can be held within a single account. In a cryptfolio, multiple cryptocurrencies can be managed as a single portfolio.

CRYPTOGRAPHY

Cryptography is the practice and study of techniques for secure communication in the presence of third parties. It is a secret code that is used to securely transmit information across non-secure communication channels, preventing anyone except the intended recipient from receiving the actual message.

CRYPTOS

Cryptos is shorthand for cryptocurrencies. The term crypto is the singular form of cryptos.

CRYPTOCURRENCIES

Cryptocurrencies are new forms of

digital currencies, led by the development of Bitcoin. These currencies use cryptography to create a secure, reliable and unalterable digital monetary system.

CURRENCY

Currency is a medium of exchange that is used by a group of people to exchange for goods and services.

FIAT CURRENCIES

Fiat currencies are government-issued currencies that have little to no commodity backing. Fiat refers to its meaning as a "decree by the government" that it has value, yet having no intrinsic value of its own. Nearly 100% of all countries in the world today have this type of currency. Many economists no longer consider fiat currencies to be true money.

FIATS

Fiats is shorthand for fiat currencies. The term fiat is the singular form of fiats.

HASH

Hash is shorthand for hash value.

HASH FUNCTION

A hash function is a cryptographic algorithm that takes as input the information to be secured and provides as output a resulting numeric value called a hash, or hash value.

HASH VALUE

A hash, or hash value, is the resulting value from a hash function.

MICRO-BITCOIN

One micro-bitcoin, or 1 μBTC, is one millionth of a bitcoin. That is, 1 BTC = 1,000,000 μBTC.

MILLI-BITCOIN

One milli-bitcoin, or 1 mBTC, is one thousandth of a bitcoin. That is, 1 BTC = 1,000 mBTC. Note also that 1 mBTC = 1,000 μBTC.

MINER

A miner is a computer that is part of the Bitcoin network that maintains the blockchain and processes new transactions as they occur. Miners do intense computational work to cryptographically secure transactions and to create new bitcoins.

MINING

Mining is the activity of processing bitcoin transactions and creating new blocks in the blockchain. This process is performed by miners who earn bitcoins as a reward for their work.

MONEY

Money is a type of currency that has intrinsic value based on the material used or the backing value associated with it. Gold and silver coins are example of currencies that have intrinsic value due to the material used to create the currency. Currency notes backed by gold or silver, such as gold or silver certificates, are examples of currencies with backing value. Both examples are considered money.

SATOSHIS

Satoshis represent the smallest units of

a bitcoin, expressed in eight decimal places. Each satoshi, the singular form of satoshis, is written as 0.00000001 BTC, or one hundred millionth of a bitcoin. That is, there are one hundred million satoshis in one bitcoin. The term satoshi is used in homage to the creator of Bitcoin, Satoshi Nakamoto.

SATOSHI NAKAMOTO

Satoshi Nakamoto, a pseudonym for one or more people, created the initial white paper that defined Bitcoin, named *Bitcoin: A Peer-to-Peer Electronic Cash System*. Satoshi Nakamoto implemented and launched Bitcoin in 2009.

TWO-FACTOR AUTHENTICATION

Two-factor authentication requires two factors, or passwords, to authenticate access. The first factor is typically a password. The second factor is frequently a one-time password (OTP) provided by SMS or by one-time password generators.

TABLES & DIAGRAMS

INDEX

10108112R00083

Printed in Great Britain
by Amazon.co.uk, Ltd.,
Marston Gate.